THE EMPIRE OF "THE CITY"

THE SECRET HISTORY OF BRITISH FINANCIAL POWER

by
E. C. KNUTH

THE BOOK TREE
San Diego, California

Originally published
1944
by E.C. Knuth
Milwaukee, Wisconsin

New material, revisions and cover
© 2006
The Book Tree
All rights reserved

ISBN 978-1-58509-262-8

Published by
The Book Tree
P O Box 16476
San Diego, CA 92176
www.thebooktree.com

We provide fascinating and educational products to help awaken the public to new ideas and
information that would not be available otherwise.
Call 1 (800) 700-8733 for our *FREE BOOK TREE CATALOG*.

ACKNOWLEDGMENTS

I wish to thank the following publishes for their courtesy in granting me permission to quote from these books:

America's Strategy in World Politics	Prof. Nicholas J. Spykman	Harcourt, Brace and Co., Inc.
Background of War	Editors of Fortune	Alfred A. Knopf, Inc.
Barriers Down	Kent Cooper	Farrar & Rinehart
The Case for India	Dr. Will Durant	Simon & Schuster, Inc.
The Day of the Saxon	Homer Lea	Harper & Brothers
From Isolation to Leadership	Prof. John H. Latane	The Odyssey Press, Inc.
The Intimate Papers of Colonel House	Prof. Chas. Seymour	Houghton Mifflin Company
Liberty-Equality-Fraternity	Dr. Nicholas Murray Butler	Chas. Scribner's Sons
The Life of W. E. Gladstone	John Morley	The MacMillan Co.
Lord Keynes, Closeup of	Noel F. Busch	Time, Inc., 1945
Merchants of Death	H. C. Engelbrecht & F. C. Hanighen	Dodd, Mead & Company
My Memories of Eighty Years	Chauncey M. Depew	Chas. Scribner's Sons
Old Diplomacy and New	A. L. Kennedy	D. Appleton-Century Co.
Pan-Americanism	Prof. Roland G. Usher	D. Appleton-Century Co.
Pan-Germanism	Prof. Roland G. Usher	Houghton Mifflin Company
"Shall It Be Again?"	John K. Turner	The Author
The United States and Great Britain	Rear Admiral Chas. L. Hussey	The University of Chicago Press
The War and Democracy	J. Dover Wilson	The MacMillan Co.

E. C. KNUTH

Member Wisconsin Society of Professional Engineers
Member National Society of Professional Engineers
Member Western Society of Engineers

INTRODUCTION TO 2ND EDITION

At the end of World War I, the writer, then 27 years old, was released from the U. S. Army as a second lieutenant of the Coast Artillery Corps. Like many more servicemen, he was filled with resentment as the deluge of utterly obvious and brazen falsehood, by which participation in that war had been forced upon the American people, was exposed, and became more evident day by day after the war was won.

That the reasons advanced to the American people for their entry into World War I were largely fraudulent became common and accepted knowledge, and over 25 years after the end of that war the eminent American historians, Charles A. and Mary R. Beard, stated in their "Basic History" (page 442) that "the gleaming mirage that pictured the World War as purely or even mainly a war for democracy and civilization dissolved beyond recognition . . .;" and the well-known Internationalist publicist, Walter Lippmann, stated in his "U. S. Foreign Policy" (page 24) in effect that the real reasons for going to war in 1917 have never been admitted.

Many people realize that this mystifying situation, in which an alleged democratic and self-governing nation is actually controlled against the will of the people in its foreign affairs, is a clear indication that there must be a very powerful and well-financed secret organization which plans and directs American foreign affairs, and for lack of a more specific identification this suspected secret organization is popularly referred to as the International Financiers.

When the propaganda mills began their characteristic grind towards war in the early 1930's, the writer began a more definite study of international power politics, and soon found it an entrancing and revealing subject. There was, however, no more free speech; and the most amazing documented aspects of a vast secret world order of International Finance could find no hearing in a situation where some Congressmen denounced overwhelming Nationalist expression of views in their mail as mere organized subversion.

The shelves of our public libraries hold thousands of books pertaining to some aspect of this vast subject; most of them dry as dust to the average reader and remaining unread by the public through the years. Most of these scholarly works are devoted to some passing phase of power politics in some part of the world, of which their author has made a specialized study, and have invariably been forgotten as the public has lost interest in that particular incident.

In running through these works some amazing nuggets of information come to light here and there, which fitted together gradually unfold the stun-

4

ning history and the legal structure of a sovereign world state located in the financial district of the loosely knit aggregation of buroughs and cities popularly known as the city of London. The colossal political and financial organization centered in this area, known as "The City," operates as a super-government of the world; and no incident occurs in any part of the world without its participation in some form.

Its pretentions are supported in the United States by the secret International Pilgrim Society, sponsor of the Cecil Rhodes "One World" ideology which was launched about 1897. The president of its American branch is Dr. Nicholas Murray Butler, who is also president of the allied Carnegie Endowment for International Peace. The ultimate objective of this camarilla was defined by one of its noted propagandists, the late William Allen White, as: "It is the destiny of the pure Aryan Anglo-Saxon race to dominate the world and kill off or else reduce to a servile status all other inferior races."

After reducing the vast mass of data forming the basis of this work into a logical and readable sequence, it was finally put into print and privately published after long delay, and copyright was granted May 22, 1944. About 200 copies were sent to various members of Congress, thus largely performing the purpose of the first edition. Several members of the Senate Foreign Relations Committee accorded some attention to this.

Senator Henrik Shipstead of Minnesota wrote August 12, 1944: "The document containing the result of your research was so interesting that it spoiled most of my sleep that night . . . I have been doing some research along the same lines and I find my time in that respect is limited. You have done a great deal of work that will save me a great deal of time." On August 21, 1944, he wrote: "People ought to be induced to read it. It is a documented piece of work and therefore should command respect and arouse interest."

This work apparently appeals most strongly to men of professional standing, and to people of the elder generations, and a number of lawyers, doctors, clergymen, architects and engineers of the writer's acquaintance have expressed their great interest and apparently general commendation. Publishers approached have been reluctant to undertake it, and several stated that there would be little demand for a serious work of this kind, as the American public is not interested in that kind of reading matter. One large Eastern publisher frankly wrote he was obliged to disregard the recommendations of his readers on advice of counsel.

Chapters I and XI, and the Conclusion, are new additions to the second edition of "The Empire of 'The City'." Chapter XI, "A Study in Power," was published separately and copyrighted February 22, 1945.

Table of Contents

THE FUNDAMENTAL BASIS OF INTERNATIONALISM

In 1912, the noted internationalist, Homer Lea, in a scientific study of basic elements of world politics, forecast as imminent and inevitable a series of gigantic world conflicts, of which World War I, World War II, and a now almost certain and nearby World War III, form a part.

Mr. Lea's great work, "The Day of The Saxon," was first published in 1912 in very limited edition, and was republished in 1942 by Harper & Brothers. It can be said to form a major book of the Internationlist "Bible," and is one of the very few works on Internationalism that treats this usually deliberately distorted subject with scholarly candor, being particularly designed for the enlightenment of the elect. The following paragraphs are selected from Chapter II of this book:

"The character of the British Dominion is different from any of the great empires that have preceded it. It not only consists of one-fourth of the land surface, but the suzerainty of the Five Seas. . . . That British rule should, in various degrees of sovereignty exercise its dominion over seventeen-twentieths of the world's surface is significant of just that degree of repression towards all other nations, their rights and expansion by land or by sea.

"Peace and its duration, like war, is determined by natural laws that in their fundamental principles do not vary nor are found wanting.

"In conformity to these laws we find that the future peace of the Empire stands in decreasing ratio and must so continue until it is either destroyed or reaches a point of world dominance.

"There can be no retention of present British sovereignty without the repression of the territorial and political expansion of other nations—a condition that must culminate in war, *one war if the Empire is destroyed; a series if it is victorious.*

"In this epoch of war upon which the Empire is about to enter, hopes of peace are futile; constitutions and kings and gods are without avail, for these are the old, old struggles that govern the growth and dissolution of national life."

This was written before the outbreak of World War I and should in the light of world events since then be very impressive. Mr. Lea states further in Chapter X: "For England to preserve to herself the balance of power in Europe, *it is necessary to limit the political and territorial expansion of any European state.*"

On page 13 of the first edition of "The Empire of 'The City' ", privately published and copyrighted 1¼ years before V-E Day, the writer predicted the coming war with Russia on the basis of the well-defined and unmistakable thread of continuity and the plainly evident pattern of the machinations of the Balance of Power by the secret British "One World" order over the past century.

The grand plan of the "One World" Order decrees that *it is necessary to limit the political and territorial expansion of Russia* PROMPTLY AND PEREMPTORILY. Otherwise the victory over Germany will be of no avail, will in fact substitute a far more dangerous and potent challenge to British sovereignty.

It was further predicted that Turkey will resume her traditional position as the spearhead in the renewal of the timeless and savage British-Russian struggle for domination, briefly interrupted since 1912 to eliminate the newly arisen German Empire and its threat to the victor. It seems likely that the coming conflict will find Finland, Latvia, Lithuania, Slovakia, Bohemia, Poland, Romania, Hungary, Austria, Servia, Greece, Turkey and Persia allied with the alleged forces of freedom.

Geopolitics, the study of the struggle for space and power, forms a well-developed science with an extensive bibliography, which conclusively impeaches the superficial fabrication, with which the American people in particular have been implanted with consummate cunning, that the great World Wars are caused by brutal attacks upon world law and order, instead of being the fully anticipated consequences of the most diabolical double dealing and planning by the secret "One World" order of "The City."

The probability of war with Russia, now highly evident and the subject of wide comment, was variously indicated and denounced as vicious and subversive propaganda at the time the 1st edition of this book went into print. As is usual, the real reasons for this very probable and nearby war are easily kept submerged because the truculence, insolence and contempt with which Russia has forestalled and checkmated the "One World" designs, with which she has had an intimate acquaintance over 130 years, fits perfectly into the sham posture of bruised democracy and violated decency.

In Chapter III of "The Prince," his great classic on the science of power, Machiavelli warns: ". . . the distempers of a State being discovered while yet inchoate (in their early stages), which can only be done by a sagacious ruler, may easily be dealt with; but when, from not being observed, they are

8

suffered to grow until they are obvious to every one, there is no longer any remedy."

Is there perhaps yet time for the Congress, ruler in this sense of the United States, to acquire the sagacity and the courage to deal with this menace of war with Russia? Is it in the public interest to expose the grand plan of the "One World" camarilla at a time when they are so near to final achievement of this plan that they need to sacrifice perhaps only ten to twenty million more lives in addition to the over one hundred million lives already sacrificed; to realize the great dream of their founder, Cecil Rhodes; a dream of a world ruled by a benevolent despotic intelligentsia, and so to create "peace for all eternity"?

The answer appears in the creed of America as defined by Thomas Jefferson "here we are not afraid to follow truth wherever it may lead, nor to tolerate any error so long as reason is left free to combat it."

How has it been possible to erect this Internationalistic structure of misrepresentation and deception in our midst and to protect it from exposure for nearly a half-century? Why have not our professors of history, our college presidents and educators, or our crusading newspapers exposed this monstrosity?

Some of the reasons are developed in the following chapters in documented detail. But there are also some evident and very practical reasons. Our newspapers are absolutely dependent for their existence on the advertising of great business interests, and perhaps the principle function of college presidents is to collect the funds upon which the existence of their institution depends, to be on the right terms with the right people.

News that definitely points to the existence of the secret world supergovernment of "The City" is treated with dense silence. The current activities of what has been identified as the most powerful international society on earth, the "Pilgrims," are so wrapped in silence that few Americans know even of its existence since 1903. As a glaring example let us consider the cross-examination of Henry Morgenthau, Jr. as to the contacts of his father with the pecular activities of the mysterious and secret British statesman Viscount Reginald Esher by Senator Gerald Nye in a Senate hearing on January 28, 1940. Apparently not one newspaper in the United States gave one inch of space to this immensely sensational exposure, while Senator Nye, like many other statesmen who have ventured too far into forbidden realms, has been effectively submerged.

As appears hereinafter, the late President David Jordan of Stanford University did much to expose the machinations of this International camarilla, with the result that he was subjected to indignity and persecution during

9

the World War I period; as was also the late Congressman Lindbergh of Minnesota, father of Colonel Charles Lindbergh.

As may be evident from the numerous quotations herein, many of the great teachers and professors of our universities have tried to throw some light into this situation with little success, for their works have been accorded little recognition, and as "controversial" matter have been treated with the contempt of silence. One source estimates the average circulation of books of this type at little over seven thousand copies.

Contrast this with the massive million copy circulations of the highly acclaimed and widely publicized products of the proponents of Internationalism; with the complete domination of the radio by Internationalist propagandists; with billion dollar funds out of the public treasury devoted to educating and informing the people; with the newspapers filled with matter supplied by foreign "information" services; with opposition controlled so as to be based on such superficial and spurious reasons as to merely help hide and detract attention from the real reasons.

The Republican Party reached such a high status in the Coolidge Admistration as the defender of Nationalism that Mr. Coolidge has been accused in some Internationalist circles of being directly responsible for the Internationalist recession which opened the way for the rebirth of Nationalism in the Totalitarian countries, among which Russia must be included. However, this Republican Nationalism has declined steadily under the encroachment of the Internationalist Money Power, so that charges of manipulation and bribery were brought after the 1940 campaign; while the candidate of 1944 was the admitted pupil of a noted Internationalist and trustee of the Carnegie Endowment for International Peace. The results of the 35 years of operation of the Carnegie Endowment for International Peace speak for themselves.

A resolution by Senator Langer, Republican Senator from North Dakota, to investigate the charge of C. Nelson Sparkes in "One Man—Wendell Willkie" that Mr. T. J. Lamont, former president of J. P. Morgan & Co. and chairman of the executive committee of the Pilgrims had bought the votes of delegates to the Republican National Convention of 1940 with a "roomful of money," was effectively submerged without any adequate public explanation.

After this brief review of recent manifestations of the parasite of foreign finance which has intertwined itself into the vitals of the capitalistic system, and which like the "Old Man of the Sea," has seated itself on the shoulders of democracy to dominate its fate, we will now turn back the pages of time 130 years to trace the development and the machinations and the structure of this octopus of power in documented step by step historical detail, as revealed by eminent scholars and writers through the years.

10

GEOPOLITICS AND THE BACKGROUND OF MODERN WARS

The events of the past ten years have brought forth a great number of books treating some aspect of Geopolitics, defined by one writer as the struggle for space and power. Among the hundreds of new works on this subject perhaps the most outstanding is "America's Strategy in World Politics," by Nicholas J. Spykman, Sterling Professor of International Relations, Yale University, published in 1942, and sponsored by The Yale Institute of International Studies. Like most books on this subject, Prof. Spykman's excellent work is very profound and comprehensive, and cannot be readily grasped by anybody not already acquainted with the outline of modern history and of modern power politics.

The modern era of world history can definitely be assumed to have had its inception with the end of the Napoleonic War because many of the problems now affecting the nations of Europe and the world in general arose out of the reconstruction of the map of the world as a result of that war. The virtual end of the Napoleonic War came with the crushing defeat of Napoleon at Leipsic in the gigantic "Battle of The Nations" in October, 1813, by the allied Russian, Austrian, Swedish and Prussian armies, followed by the abdication of Napoleon and his banishment to Elba in April, 1814.

Prof. Spykman describes the British policies in foreign affairs, which he alleges have earned her the designation of "Perfidious Albion," in his treatment of "Britain and the Balance of Power" (pages 103 to 107). He develops the British policy as a constant succession of cycles of shift partners, isolation, alliance and war; and the defeat of Napoleon marked the end of one of these cycles. A tabulation of the modern wars of the world which follows immediately herein, and which assumes the Napoleonic War as modern cyclical war No. 1, would indicate the present war as cyclical war No. 7, and very possibly as cyclical war No. 1 of a new grand cycle.

In his "Conclusion" (pages 446-472), Prof. Spykman ventures the opinion that Britain cannot permit a complete German defeat as that would leave the European continent in the grip of Russia; and that she cannot permit a full Japanese defeat as that would leave Asia in the grip of an awakened and revitalized China. He is further very doubtful of a complete world hegemony by some type of British-American union, and concludes that only Japan would be able to supply the missing weight. Thus, strangely, Prof. Spykman would restore the overwhelming power of the alliance of the imperialistic expansion of 1897-1920, when Europe was in balance by the British alliance with France, Asia was in balance by the British alliance with Japan, and the world was in balance by the British alliance with the United States under the secret agreement of 1897.

One of the most forthright revelations, both of the secret agreement of 1897 and of the malignant disease which underlies modern civilization, and which threatens to tumble the world back into chaos and barbarism, was disclosed in a speech by Chauncey M. Depew, New York Senator and high political and financial power of his day, in seconding the nomination of Theodore Roosevelt for the Vice-Presidency of the United States at the Republican National Convention of 1900, when he stated in part: "What is the tendency of the future? Why this war in South Africa? Why this hammering at the gates of Pekin? Why this marching of troops from Asia to Africa? Why these parades of people from other empires to other lands? It is because the surplus productions of the civilized countries of modern times are greater than civilization can consume. It is because this overproduction goes back to stagnation and poverty. The American people now produce two thousand million dollars' worth more than we can consume, and we have met the emergency; and by the providence of God, by the statesmanship of William McKinley, and by the valor of Roosevelt and his associates, we have our market in the Philippines, and we stand in the presence of eight hundred millions of people, with the Pacific as an American lake . . ."

In the following tabulation the modern cyclical wars of the British Empire in its unceasing struggle to maintain control of the dynamic and rapidly shifting balance of world power are numbered in order, while the intermediate cyclical or pivotal wars are indicated by the letter O, and the wars of imperialistic expansion by the letter X:

Cyclical wars and Imperialistic wars	Major Powers allied with British Empire	Major British opponents
No. 1—Napoleonic War 1793-1815	England, Prussia, Sweden, Russia and Austria	France.
2—Turkish War 1827-1829	England, France and Russia	Turkey and Egypt.
3—Crimean War 1853-1856	England, France, Turkey and Sardinia	Russia
O—Civil War 1861-1865	England, France, Spain and Confederate States	Russia, (Prussia) and United States
O—Franco-Prussian 1870-1871	France, (England and Austro-Hungary)	Germany, (Russia and Italy)
4—Russian-Turkish 1877-1878	Turkey, England, (France) and (Austro-Hungary)	Russia and (Germany)
X—Egyptian War 1882-1885	England, France and (Austro-Hungary)	Egypt, (Turkey and Russia)

12

(Era of imperialistic expansion under the wing of the overwh̶
British-French-American-Japanese alliance of 1897-1920.)

Cyclical wars and Imperialistic wars	Major Powers allied with British Empire	Major British opponents
No. 5—Spanish-American 1898-1899	United States and (England)	Spain and (Germany)
X—Sudan War 1898-1899	England	Sudanese-Egyptian Nationalists
X—Boer War 1899-1902	England	Orange Free State and South African Rep
X—Partition of Siam 1899-1909	England and France	Siamese Nationalists
O—Russian-Japanese 1904-1905	Japan (and England)	Russia (and Germany)
X—Morocco Conflict 1904-1906	"The Allies" (and Italy)	Germany and Austro-Hungary
X—Persian Conflict 1907-1912	England (and France)	Russia and (Germany)
O—Morocco "Affair" 1911	England and France	Germany
O—Tripoli War 1911-1912	Italian "reward" or "material quid pro quo"	Turkey
O—1st Balkan War 1912-1913	Greece, Serbia, Bulgaria and Montenegro	Turkey
O—2nd Balkan War 1913	Rumania, Greece and Serbia	Bulgaria
6—World War I 1914-1918	"The Allies" and Italy, Rumania, Greece, Serbia, Montenegro, etc. (Pop. 1,200,000,000)	Germany, Austro-Hungary Turkey, and Bulgaria. (Pop. 120,000,000)

(The era of imperialistic expansion, inaugurated by the internationalistic William McKinley, Chauncey M. Depew and Theodore Roosevelt of the party of "The Full Dinner Pail" of 1896, was ended in 1920 when the people of the United States buried the interventionist candidates on the Democratic ticket of that year, James E. Cox and Franklin Delano Roosevelt, under a gigantic landslide.)

(The alliance with the British Empire was resumed with the election of the party of "The More Abundant Life.")

No. O—South American Conflict and World-wide boycott 1934-1939	"The Allies"	Germany
7—World War II 1939-? (World War II appears to be cyclical war No. 1 of a new Grand Cycle)	"The Allies" (Pop. 1,100,000,000)	Germany, Japan, Hungary, Roumania, Bulgaria, Slovakia, Finland, (Italy), (France), and (Spain) with subject areas (Pop. 700,000,000)
New Cycle No. 2—Russian seizure of Warm Water Ports	"The Allies", Turkey, etc.	Russia and new Soviet states

13

as here used refers to diplomatic intrigue, incitations
id military and naval demonstrations and clashes
mes of countries shown in parenthesis indicate allies
ry into war, due to limited length of the conflict or
or paired with a major opponent. The same indi-
indicate the present doubtful position of Italy and
France.

The predicted clash with Russia, within this decade of the British allies, assisted by Turkey, seems an utterly logical conclusion. Every Russian diplomatic move and every Russian war for one hundred thirty years has been a part of a campaign, which has cost many millions of lives, to reach Constantinople and the Dardanelles. The price exacted by Russia for her entry into World War I was Constantinople, the city of the Tsar, the city of the Caesar, the Tsarigrad. World War II has a very surprising resemblance to almost every aspect of the colossal Napoleonic struggle, and the ground-work is apparently being laid to repeat the bloody 130 year grand cycle here outlined.

China, Russia, the United States and Germany are in order the most populous independent nations in the world, and therefore represent the most dynamic and most dangerous competition of the British Empire. All of them have been the victims of recurrent British repression. The Russian and German cycles of repression were listed in the foregoing tabulation. The Chinese cycle follows:

War and Period	British Allies	British Opponent
Opium War, 1840-1843	England and France	Chinese Dynasty
Revolution, 1857-1858	England and France	Chinese Nationalists
Storming of Pekin, 1860	England and France	Chinese Dynasty
Revolution, 1860-1865	England and France	Chinese Nationalists
Yellow War, 1894-1895	Japan and (England)	Chinese Dynasty
Revolution, 1898	England-France-Japan	Chinese Nationalists
Boxer War, 1900-1901	All the Great Powers	Chinese Nationalists
Revolution, 1911	England-France-Japan	Chinese Nationalists
Revolution, 1926-1927	England, France, Japan, Portugal, Spain and Holland	Gen. Chiang Kai-shek
Manchurian Conquest, 1931	Japan	Gen. Chiang Kai-shek

Of the events which led to the British war with the Chinese Nationalists under Chiang Kai-Shek in 1926-1927, T'ang Leang-Li writes in "China in Revolt" published in London in 1927 that the City of Wanhsien of 750,000 population was bombarded on Sunday evening, Sept. 5, 1926, by a British fleet, causing civilian casualties of 2000 and destruction of a great part of the city. This despite the fact that General Yang Sen had merely detained the British steamer Wanliu to investigate a "river outrage" and negotiations had been in progress a day or two, and despite the fact that bombardment

14

of an unfortified town is forbidden by international law. The bombardment was made the subject of a message of congratulation to the naval authority by H. M. Government.

T'ang Leang-Li further charges that repeated raids on the Kuo Min Tang headquarters in the British Concession at Tientsin, in November and December of the year before, by the British police, resulting in the handing over of numerous Nationalists, including several girl students, for court-martial to their mortal enemies, who are notoriously savage in their dealings with political opponents, cannot but be interpreted as a desire on the part of the British authorities at Tientsin to assist in a plain and deliberate massacre; that British agents in China continue to pursue the traditional policy of blackmail and bully. The British policy of the Iron Hand, far from intimidating the Chinese people, has as its effect the rallying of the Chinese masses to the banner of the anti-Imperialist Chinese National Party. (Page 156.)

T'ang Leang-Li describes in some detail the spider-web of exploitation woven about China by International Finance, and the traditional British policy of promptly attacking and eradicating any Chinese government indicating initiative and growing strength.

Few Americans realize that as late as 1932, Japan was engaged in subduing Manchuria as a British ally, with British support and protection, against the protests of the League of Nations, the United States and China.

Manchuria was awarded to Japan by the British international financial oligarchy for assuming the greater part of the fighting and the expense to overcome the Chinese Nationalist revolution of 1926-1927 under General Chiang Kai-shek against the domination of the British. It is of interest to note that every war listed as a "Revolution," including the "Boxer" War, was a war against foreign imperialists holding the Chinese Government in bondage, a war against the bankers of the City and against the "foreign devils."

The statesmen of the international financial oligarchy made many deceptive and illusory promises to many peoples and many nations before and during World War I to induce them to fight their aggressors and to defeat them in absolute and total victory, and Mr. Woodrow Wilson promised many more things, and these promises were revoked almost without exception after total victory had been won. Mr. Wilson's promises of "New Orders" and "New Freedoms" to the subjects of the British Empire were all retracted and resulted in an immense wave of riot and revolution over a period of years following World War I. The following are some of the most outstanding of these instances of bloodshed:

15

Egyptian Revolution....................1919 - 1921
Anglo-Irish War.............Jan., 1919 - May, 1921
Ulster War...................July, 1920 - June, 1922
Massacre of Amritsar................April 13, 1921
Indian Revolution......................1921 - 1922
Egyptian Revolution....................1924 - 1925

In an editorial "A Dwarf Between Giants" in the Chicago Tribune of Sunday February 6, 1944, appears a statement that the British Foreign office has generally run America's foreign affairs for fifty years, and that for the past eleven years the British have had no difficulty in guiding our policy. That this is true is apparent from the following chapters herein in which is given a detailed description of the means, the men, and the methods by which this was accomplished.

III

THE EASTERN QUESTION

The end of the Napoleonic war left the mighty Turkish Empire form-ing a great crescent directly across the path to India. At that time Turkey included much of what is now Jugo-Slavia, Greece, Roumania, Bulgaria, and northern Africa up to Tunis and it was a potent threat to further British expansion in the Mohammedan East. An uprising in the Greek provinces of Turkey provided a suitable cause for war. Russia joined the British-French alliance as the protector of her brethren of the Greek Catholic Church and in promotion of her aspiration to gain access to open water through the Porte. A British-French-Russian fleet destroyed an allied Turkish-Egyptian fleet on Oct. 20, 1827. Then the British and French withdrew, leaving Russia to fight Turkey alone. Russia defeated the Turks and the war was ended on Sept. 24, 1829.

The British and French would not permit Russia the fruits of victory; she was not permitted to open the Porte or to gain free access to open water, and her efforts for over one hundred years up to this day to gain unrestricted access to a warm water port through the Porte, the Baltic, the Persian Gulf or the Yellow Sea have been frustrated by the "policy of encirclement," and this subject will come up for troublesome discussion in the near future.

After having been reduced to utter bankruptcy, inflation and despair by the frightful bloodletting of the gigantic Napoleonic World War, the new French Government was readily subsidized by the International Bankers in an alliance which made France the perennial junior partner in their world imperialism for over one hundred years until the recent collapse of France. France has been the ideal partner for she has always conceded to the Lion, "the Lion's share;" a share which has always been about 75% or over, even in the case of World War I.

Several million Greek Orthodox Christians still remained under Turkish rule after Russia had achieved the independence of Greece in 1829, and these people were subjected to the most inhuman and monstrous cruelties by Mohammedan persecution; and this condition continued over a long span of years until modern times, despite repeated promises of reform by the Turkish Government. As the Czar considered himself the protector of these Greek Orthodox Christians, this provided a constant cause of friction and grievance, which together with the British and Turkish obstruction to the Russian pressure for free passage through the Porte, was known as "The Eastern Question;" and this situation overshadowed the power politics of Europe for almost three quarters of a century and formed the basis for a succession of bloody conflicts.

The Standard History, 1899, quotes:- "The ascendancy of Russia was accompanied by the rise of a wholly new policy in Europe with regard to the Eastern Question. The old feeling that the Turk was the common enemy of Christendom, that every victory over the Crescent, no matter by what power it was gained, was a subject for general triumph, completely disappeared. On the contrary, the Turkish power was to be maintained, because Russia was dreaded."

Britain resurrected the principle laid down by William Pitt who had argued that "the true principle by which the foreign policy of England should be directed, was the fundamental principle of preserving the balance of power in Europe; and that the true doctrine of the balance of power required that the Russian Empire should not, if possible, be allowed to increase, nor that of Turkey to diminish."

Twenty-four years after Russia had helped Britain overcome the menace of the Mussulman to her eastern possessions, the first war broke in the "Eastern Question;" the great Crimean War, in which Britain, France and Turkey (later joined by Sardinia, predecessor of modern Italy) defeated Russia in 1853-1856 at a cost of one million lives. The House of Savoy, rulers of Sardinia, entered this war in a political deal which placed it on the throne of a newly united Italy in 1861, through British victory.

The years of 1869-70 found Britain and its balance of power in an exceedingly precarious position. Its interference in the American Civil War now faced it with an angry and resentful America possessed of the world's greatest army and a powerful navy of the new and terrible ironclads, demanding redress for heavy damages due to British lend-lease to the Confederacy. Russia had fully signified her intention to fight for revenge of her beating in the war of 1853-1856 by sending two fleets to the United States when war had seemed most imminent between the United States and Britain during the Civil War, and in a further incident of strange significance, the Queen of Spain was dethroned in a revolution.

This auspicious moment was seized by Prussia, largest of the many small German speaking states of central Europe, to abandon her role in the local politics of Europe and to enter on the stage of world power politics. Her ambitious prime-minister, Count von Bismarck, had already unified the German states into a loose confederation, and now attempted to place a Prussian princeling on the vacant throne of Spain. This was a step towards a natural alliance, for Spain was and still is the implacable and unforgiving foe of Britain, the nation that seized its colonies and reduced it to a state of poverty and decay.

The move of Bismarck to place a German ruler on the throne of Spain was summarily challenged by France and the name of the German candidate, Prince Leopold of Hohenzollern-Sigmaringen, was withdrawn within about ten days by July 12, 1870. In accordance with the established tradition of the British-French financial oligarchy never to accept anything short of unconditional surrender, the French government demanded in addition an abject personal apology from King William I of Prussia on July 14, 1870.

When this personal apology was refused France declared war the following day. Britain, as usual, made no immediate move; and six months and twelve days later, on January 27, 1871, the defeat of France was utter and complete. Nearly all the German States promptly joined in the war, and by the end of July, the highly skilled German military chief, General von Moltke, had 700,000 men along the French frontier. Emperor Napoleon III took over the chief command of the French armies. Napoleon III was captured by the Germans together with 120,000 men at the Battle of Sedan, on Sept. 2, 1870. On January 19, 1871, King William I of Prussia, was formally proclaimed Emperor of the new German Empire, a union of four kingdoms and twenty-one other principalities of central Europe. Although the war had been very short, nearly one-half million men perished. (See footnote.)

A message was transmitted for the French Emperor on July 5, 1870, by Baron Rothschild of Paris to Baron Lionel Nathan Rothschild of London. The message was deciphered by Nathaniel Maier Rothschild, still head of the House of Rothschild at the beginning of World War I, and by him delivered to Mr. Gladstone early on the morning of July 6th. The message was to inform Mr. G. that the council of ministers at Madrid had decided to propose Prince Leopold of Hohenzollern for the Spanish throne, that his candidature would be intolerable to France, that the Emperor hoped Mr. Gladstone would endeavor to secure its withdrawal.

Mr. Gladstone stated his reluctance to interfere with the liberty of the Spanish people to choose their own sovereign. He was nevertheless later confronted with a dispatch to the King of Prussia drafted by Lord Granville and asked to sign the same. Again Mr. Gladstone was reluctant, but after several days of hesitation, he added to Lord Granville's draft an appeal to the magnanimity of the King, begged him to consider the danger to the peace of Europe, enjoined him further to say nothing to give ground for the supposition that England had any business to discuss the abstract right of Spain to choose her own sovereign. (*Morley's Life of G., Book VI, Ch. IV.*)

Gladstone's appeal was supported by an energetic representation to Berlin by Austria, seat of the third Rothschild dynasty, and the King of Prussia immediately ordered the candidacy of Prince Leopold withdrawn. Having inveigled Mr. Gladstone into a definite position, the tone of France suddenly became harsh and menacing. Evidently mistaking the quick compliance of King William I as a sign of weakness and fear of an apparently united Austrian, British and French coalition, they demanded two days later, on July 14th, that the Prussian King make a personal pledge that he would never again sanction any similar political move. This was an ultimatum of unparalleled effrontery demanding in effect that Prussia in utter humiliation acknowledge herself a vassal of France, with no further voice in the council of Nations. The King politely declined the French demand and France declared war the next day. Each and every war of modern times has been preceded by an interchange in similar terms of arrogance and contempt by the statesmen allied with

19

This war occured in the adult life of thousands of American citizens of today; and in that same span from 1871 to today perhaps 25,000,000 to 30,000,000 human beings have lost their lives in the struggle of the "Balance of Power." This is a "Big-League" game, and we are now the principal participant.

The crash of the European Balance of Power was promptly exploited to its utmost by the nations of the continent. The head of the House of Savoy revoked the agreement with the British-French oligarchy by which he had been made King of Italy and sent an army to seize the Pontifical States of Italy, which were under the temporal rule of the Pope as their absolute sovereign. The troops of the Pope surrendered on September 20, 1870, and the capital of Italy was moved from Florence to Rome on July 3, 1871.

Russia at the outbreak of this war denounced the treaty of 1856 and rebuilt her Black Sea fleet and fortifications, and prepared to resume her offensive in the "Eastern Question," thus undoing everything for which a million men had died a brief 15 years before. She had openly supported Prussia and any move on the part of England would have promptly brought her into the Franco-Prussian war, and she now was free to act. Her first move was a drive into Turkestan up to the borders of Persia, Afghanistan and India. In this campaign she defeated the Khan of Khiva in the spring of 1873, the Turkomans in the fall of 1873, and the Khan of Khokand in the summer of 1875.

In the meantime Russian political penetration roused the peasants of the Turkish provinces of Herzegovina and Bosnia into rebellion in July, 1875, and this was followed by declarations of war by other Turkish political subdivisions; Servia and Montenegro in 1876, and Bulgaria and Roumania in 1877. The stage was then set for Russia's answer to the Eastern Question and her revenge for the horrors perpetrated on her religious compatriots, and the war that followed was fought with bestial fury, with no quarter given or asked. The Turks fought with frenzied determination and losses were immense on both sides, but the odds were too great and nine months after

---

International Finance; with a disdainful refusal of any basis of settlement making any reasonable concession.

Gladstone was horrified; and this great opponent of Toryism and its wars stated that the diplomacy on the side of the Government of France anterior to the war, made up a chapter which for fault and folly taken altogether is almost without a parallel in the history of nations. With one stroke France united the quarreling and jealous small German kingdoms and principalities of central Europe into a great empire and threw itself under the grinding wheels of Bismarck, to be utterly demolished in six months time. The French calculations proved entirely wrong. The illusion of International Finance that Russia had been immobilized for 100 years by the Crimean War of only 14 years before quickly vanished, with a vindicative Russia holding Austria at bay and repudiating her terms of surrender in that war. The German victory was too sudden to permit the financiers of the City and the Conservatives to unseat the anti-imperialistic Liberal, Gladstone; and to intervene.

declaration of war the Russian army was encamped in the suburbs of Constantinople, with the Turkish army totally dispersed. The Russians had been well prepared, for two immense armies totalling 500,000 men had moved over the border into Turkey within a few hours after the declaration of war.

The conduct of this war throughout was exceedingly brutal. Turkish prisoners were kept herded out in the open in bitter winter weather without food or shelter for many days, to die by the thousands. The American military observer, Lieut. F. V. Greene, relates in "Army Life in Russia," published in 1881 that in passing one of the burial trenches filled with the bodies of naked Turkish dead, he saw among the corpses a living man; his head and one arm only visible, speechlessly beckoning for aid. He called attention to this man but nothing was done for him. Nevertheless, when the Russians reached the suburbs of Constantinople, they did not enter the city to loot and destroy; on the contrary, the Grand Duke Nikolaus made a formal call on the Sultan to pay his respects, duly returned by the Sultan.

A treaty of peace was made at San Stefano, near Constantinople, on March 3, 1878, between Russia and Turkey; which was promptly challenged by Disraeli. Britain had been unable to come to Turkey's assistance, but had charged Russia with deliberate violation of the Treaty of Paris in attacking the integrity of the Ottoman Empire. To save face, she declared she would remain neutral as long as British interests were not attacked, and these were defined as follows: First, the navigation of the Suez Canal must not be blockaded or interfered with. Second, Egypt must not be attacked or occupied. Third, Constantinople must not pass into any other hands than those of its present possessors. Fourth, the existing arrangements concerning the navigation of the Bosphorus and the Dardanelles must not be changed.

Unable to oppose Russia by force, Britain appealed the Treaty of San Stefano to the Concert of Europe, an informal organization of the nations of Europe which had attempted to install a system of law and order into the affairs of the world since the Napoleonic wars. Russia obediently waited on the outskirts of Constantinople for six months after the close of the war; her soldiers eager to go home after their great victory, ill-housed and exposed to the weather and ravaged by disease, until the European Concert had concluded the Treaty of Berlin on July 13, 1878.

That part of the Eastern Question pertaining to the Turkish atrocities was now fully settled with general freedom for the Balkan nations, and Russia had demolished the Porte; but, on the other side of the Porte stood the British fleet, and that part of the Eastern Question has never been settled, for the new alignments of the Balance of Power left Russia helpless in Europe thereafter.

With their Turkish ally of no further use, the British banking oligarchy subsidized the government of Turkey's vassal state Egypt the next year with a largely fictitious loan. The Egyptians rose against this seizure under the leadership of their War Minister Arabi Pasha with the battle cry of "Egypt for the Egyptians." While the French and British fleets demolished the Egyptian fleet in July 1882 and defeated Arabi's army shortly afterwards, the revolution continued for many years. In 1885, the renowned "trouble shooter" of the British Empire, Gen. Chas. G. Gordon lost his life in the Egyptian war, and final victory was not achieved by the British until 1898, when Lord Kitchener defeated the Mahdi. Gen. Gordon, also known as Gordon Pasha and as Chinese Gordon, played a large role in the British and French subjugation of China.

Turkey, once the world's greatest empire, and still the nominal leader of the vast Mohammedan world, has had a number of years of fair prosperity and modernization and has profited much from the present war. The Mohammedans, largely under British and French rule, have a great store of grievances against this rule, real and fancied; and with the relatively small Christian white population of the world engaged in annihilating themselves in a shambles of intolerance caused by illusion and deceit; a world-wide uprising of the Mussulman is not so far-fetched.

IV

THE CONCERT OF EUROPE

The leading powers of Europe had adopted a custom of meeting in a conference from time to time whenever some particularly perplexing problem arose to threaten the peace, and the successive treaties and agreements adopted at these conventions in time covered a large part of the customs and intercourse between these nations. This concert of the nations in time assumed an official status. The effect of this was to create a type of "League of Nations;" which, while not in itself an entity, nevertheless ruled by the will of the majority.

Among the earlier meetings of the Powers were the Congress of Vienna in 1814-1815, of Aix-la-Chapelle in 1818, Carlsbad in 1819, Verona in 1822, and London in 1830. The Concert of Europe attempted again and again to bring about a settlement in the Eastern Question. Only British consent kept the Congress from quickly disposing of that part of the Eastern Question affecting the Mohammedan persecution of the millions of Christians of the Turkish conquered Balkan nations, by united action of all the nations of continental Europe. These small nations had been conquered by the Turk after the Christian world had collapsed due to economic causes similar to those of the past few years and a frantic new deal type of spending, which had eventually exhausted the inexhaustible treasury of Rome, that great empire which included nearly all of Europe, present-day Turkey, and other parts of Asia and Africa.

Civilization has risen to great peaks and fallen to deep valleys again and again during the centuries, and Rome marked the last great peak of civilization. Let us note that Rome built 50,000 miles of hard-surfaced cement roads in its day; that for one thousand years after the fall of Rome not one mile of cement road was built in Europe, that even the secret of making cement was only rediscovered in recent years. That with its capital spent, all Europe plunged into chaos, with its immense natural wealth of little avail.

That inexorable self-interest which will sacrifice everything and anything to the future expansion and well-being of the British Empire was clearly and shamelessly exposed in every discussion of the Eastern Question during the years. The traditional British explanation of their war aims, originated in her war with France for hegemony of the seas of the world, that it was not their intent to fight the French people—only to rid Europe of the Scourge of Napoleon, bring peace to Europe and preserve the rights of small nations; since repeated in war after war with a slight transposition of names, was not used in this instance. Every aspect of human decency, of human compassion, of the freedom of men, of the rights of small nations, left British statesmen cold, were championed entirely by Russia. Ghoulish atrocities committed under that command of the Koran: "O true believers, wage war against such of the infidels as are near you," were loftily ignored in expediency of empire; nothing was to be permitted to upset the then secure Balance of Power.

In treating the Eastern Question in his "Army Life in Russia," Lieut. F. V. Greene, the former military attache to the U. S. Legation at St. Petersburg wrote: "Deprived of her colonies and her commerce, England would at once sink to the level of the smaller states of Europe, following in the wake of Holland and Venice and Spain, who in their days have been great and powerful, but who have declined with the loss of their foreign possessions and the commerce which they sustained. . . . No single event could strike so serious a blow as the loss of India. Of all the great possessions—it is hardly a colony—it is the most alien to the British race, and it is held as a mere money-making investment. Its people are ground with extortionate taxation, are allowed no voice in their own affairs, are treated with studied scorn. . . . It is held as a market in which to buy cheap and sell dear, and as a place in which younger sons and needy relations can amass fortunes to be subsequently enjoyed in England. Its loss would result in a financial crisis which would shake the whole fabric of England's commercial prosperity, and deal a blow at her political prestige from which she could hardly recover."

Lieut. Greene stated further in this book:- "I have also attempted to give prominence to the Russian views of the question—which, in the main, I believe to the correct ones—because Americans are in the habit of hearing only the other side. Our language being the same as that of England, and the opinions of the Continent being transmitted to us principally through the English press, we receive constantly the most prejudiced, unfair, and at times false statements about Eastern affairs." Of the diplomatic discussions over the Turkish revolutions which immediately preceded Russian intervention he wrote: "Austria, Germany, France and Italy all in turn pressed England to accept the memorandum, or to suggest any modifications she might desire in its language. She declined to do either. They then asked Lord Derby if he had any proposition of his own to make, and he replied none. "Her Majesty's Government deprecated the diplomatic action of the other Powers in the affairs of the Ottoman Empire." Russia then asked what was the drift of England's policy; what were her ideas in the matter? To which Lord Derby replied, that he thought nothing remained but to let the struggle continue until success should declare itself on one side or the other. In other words, in British phrase, form a ring and let 'em fight it out with the usual result of indiscriminate slaughter and pillage . . ."

The political aims of nations change little through the years, and one hundred years in the life of a nation are perhaps as ten in the life of the individual. That the leopard did not change his spots in the case of Britain would appear from the fact that Sir Edward Grey used these tactics of the Lord Derby almost exactly in evading the urgent representations of Germany in her effort to escape World War I in 1914, as recorded by J. Ramsay Mac-Donald, later Prime Minister of Britain, in his article "Why We Are At War. A Reply to Sir Edward Grey," in which he accused Sir Edward Grey of the war guilt. It is utterly impossible to reconcile these lofty and disdainful expressions of Lord Derby with the crushing debacle that followed at once when Russia removed Turkey from the British Balance of Power with one ferocious lunge, thus disproving the view of many Englishmen that the march of Russian conquest had been set back one hundred years by the Crimean War of only 21 years before.

Surprised and frightened Britain now turned to the Concert of Europe, which she had heretofore flouted, for assistance. The British-French financial oligarchy had been grooming Austria for some years as a British ally in the growing German and Russian menace through their related banking house at Vienna. To influence the Congress of Berlin in its consideration of the Treaty of Stefano, it was threatened to have Austria attack Russia with British financial support. In addition British reserves were called out. War-weary Russia was obliged to accept new terms and the Treaty of Berlin signed July 13, 1878, deprived her of any territorial gain, but allowed her an indemnity for part of her war cost. In general, the freedom of the Balkan nations was admitted with various modifications to remove their governments from any Russian influence. Armenia was left under Turkish rule to furnish another Eastern Question in very recent years. Herzegovina and Bosnia whose rebellion in July 1875 had started this era of bloody slaughter, were given to Austria for her support of Britain over their furious protests; and it was rebellion in these provinces of Austria which touched off the fuse in World War I, 36 years after they had become Austrian provinces. Britain seized Cyprus in order to create a base to halt any further designs by Russia upon the Porte.

All the nations of Europe now considered the Eastern Question fully settled and Russia also realized the futility of any further efforts in the face of the new powers. Europe had assumed its modern complexion, with the new "Great Powers" of Germany, Italy and Austria-Hungary in full strength. The successful settlement of the Eastern Question had raised the Concert of Europe to the status of the de facto government of the world. The British Balance of Power was in abeyance, and there was an era of stablity. Germany in particular engaged in no major conflict for 43 years.

25

V

THE EUROPEAN CONCERT ENDS IN THE EAST

Immediately after the Russo-Turkish war the British-French oligarchy was engaged for some years in the conquest of the former Turkish vassal state Egypt and the Egyptian Sudan, but their world-wide program of aggression and expansion was badly curtailed by the restrictions imposed by the Congress of Europe, which had extended its sphere of influence to cover the entire world. There was a continual pressure, sometimes referred to as piracy, on the part of the great European members of the Concert for equivalent compensation for every other nation for each British-French penetration and expansion, and a growing fleet of a powerful Germany was a particularly insistent persuader and irritant in this attitude.

This irksome situation of general interference in the affairs of the British-French financial house was aggravated by the threat of revolution in many of its colonies, and the most dangerous of these revolutions was threatening in China about 1894. China had been subjected to British-French commercial and political control in the Opium War of 1840 (see footnote). Since that time there had been a succession of uprisings of the Chinese Nationalists to throw off this yoke. The British and French were obliged to fight this Chinese aggression in 1840 to 1843, from 1857 to 1858, from 1860 to 1865, in 1894, in 1898, in 1900, in 1911 and in 1927; in addition to almost endless minor aggression in one part of China or another. For this aggression China had indemnities assessed against her which ranged from about $28,750,000.00 in 1843 to $750,000,000.00 in 1900. The government of China in 1894 was in the hands of a British mercenary, Li Hung-Chang, a former lieutenant of the noted British "trouble-shooter" Chinese Gordon, who ruled as Vice-Roy.

This brewing and most certain revolution was known to be well organized and together with the growing pressure of the European Concert for a more equitable participation and distribution of the raw materials and resources of the world, faced the international oligarchy with a rapidly growing menace abroad at a time when the Gladstone Liberals were still loud and vocal and unmuzzled. While Mr. Gladstone had been openly charged with treason for

---

Of the opium War of 1840 Mr. William E. Gladstone said: "I am not competent to judge how long this war may last . . . but that I can say, that a war more unjust in its origin, a war more calculated in its progress to cover this country with disgrace, I do not know and I have not read of."

his opposition to British imperialistic aggression; the benign character of that dual and double-headed Dr. Jekyl and Mr. Hyde structure of government, known to Americans simply as the British Government, was still at one of its peaks of strength; and the financial oligarchy found itself in a very weak and vulnerable position, in dealing with the imminent Chinese uprising.

Of this concealed dual nature of the British Government, George Burton Adams, late Professor of History, Emeritus, Yale University, authoritatively develops in his "Constitutional History of England" that the members of the British Cabinet are strangely impotent; are not permitted to make any written notations of proceedings of the Cabinet; have no access to records of proceedings, if any, made by the Prime Minister; are not permitted to make reference afterwards to anything that had transpired at a meeting of the Cabinet (page 493). He further develops the utter lack of power of the House of Commons and of the House of Lords (pages 472-474); states "The House of Commons no longer controls the Executive; on the contrary the Executive controls the House of Commons." (Page 495.) There is a distinction between the Government of Great Britain, which is largely confined to the internal government of the British Isles, and the British Government which controls the British Empire.

Referring to "Great Britain, Banking In" in the Encyclopedia Americana, it appears that the Bank of England is not subject to any control by any governmental agency of Great Britain, and that it is above all government, despite the fact that it is *privately owned* and its directors are nominated by its proprietors. In the Encyclopedia Britannica of 1891 it is termed "a great Engine of Government." It is obvious that this privately owned foreign institution is now in grave financial difficulties with its loans and bonds and mortgages disavowed all over the world, and that it is being bolstered by huge funds being syphoned into it out of the treasury of the United States. (See footnote.)

The 1943 edition of the Encyclopedia Americana (Vol. 13) makes this stunningly significant statement of the Bank of England, that full partner of the American Administration in the conduct of the financial affairs of all the world: ". . . Its weakness is the weakness inherent in a system which has developed with the smallest amount of legislative control . . . its capital is held privately, and its management is not in any way directly or indirectly controlled by the state. On the other hand, during its whole history, it has been more or less under the protection of the state; its development has been marked by successive loans of its capital to the state in return for the confirmation or extension of its privileges, and it still continues to exercise powers and owe responsibilities delegated by the state . . . The bank of England is controlled by a governor, deputy-governor and a court of 24 directors *who are elected by the proprietors* on the nomination of the directors . . ." (This is a description of a privately owned structure of government, sovereign in its own right, and over and above the laws of England. A status admittedly attained by bribing dishonest officials of the Government of the British Isles through the years to gradually extinguish the freedom and rights of the people.)

That the nature of this strange bank is actually that of a secret holding company of colossal size is indicated by a reference in "England's Money Lords Tory M. P.", by Simon Haxey, to (page 158) Lancastshire Steel Corporation, subsidiary of the Bank of England.

The startling aspect of the dual nature of the British Government has the support of many eminent authorities on the subject, despite the fact that millions of American school textbooks and works of popular reference, and the books of thousands of pseudo history experts, have woven a fabric of deceit, and created popular acceptance of an illusion and a fallacy by the cumulative force of constant repetition.

The impeachment of this dual structure of government by Prof. Adams is fully supported by the authoritative "Laws of England" of the Lord of Halsbury, a massive work of many huge volumes, and by the specific statements and writings of David Starr Jordan, late president of Stanford University, Gladstone, David Lloyd George, J. Ramsay MacDonald, Vincent C. Vickers, director of the Bank of England and of Vickers-Armstrong armament works, Harold J. Laski and many others. "Better Times" by the Hon. D. Lloyd George in 1910 is particularly revealing. (See footnote.)

The wide latitude of action of the agents and servants of the CROWN and their remarkable immunity from the interference of English Courts and of English law appears in the "Laws of England" of Lord Halsbury as apparent from a few selected passages as follows: Vol. 6, page 388, art. 582— . . . Nor can the Crown, by proclamation or otherwise, make or unmake any law on its own authority apart from Parliament, except in colonies to which representative institutions have not been granted. (This excepts only England, Canada, Australia, Union of South Africa and New Zealand, who between them have only 13%—almost the total white population of 68,000,000 of the Empire—of the people of the British Empire, from the utterly absolute and autocratic rule of the Crown, THE Bank and THE City.)

Vol. 23, page 307, par. 641 — If under a treaty with a foreign state, a government has received funds for the benefit of a private person or class of persons, although a moral obligation may thereby be imposed upon the government to pay the funds so received to such persons, no action or petition of right, will be at their suit to recover the fund, and the intended ultimate beneficiaries cannot compel the government to carry out the obligation.

Par. 642 — An executive or administrative act of a subject, though in the first instance done without the authority of his Sovereign, will have all the effect of an Act of State if subsequently ratified. (This provides the facilities to make the law afterwards to fit the case, as developed by Prof. Edwin J. Clapp in "Economic Aspects of the War" published 1915 as having been the procedure in the matter of the American ship Wilhelmina.)

Par. 643 — The Sovereign can do no wrong, and no legal proceedings can be brought against him . . .

Par. 648 — As regards Ireland, all of the official acts of the Lord Lieutenant are Acts of State apparently even if ultra vires (transcending authority conferred by law).

Par. 650 — The official acts of every state or potentate whose independence has been recognized by the Crown, and of their authorized agents, are Acts of State. No action can be brought in respect of such acts, even where the agent is a British subject, and where, in carrying out the Act of State, he is committing an offense against English law . . .

This gives a fair outline of the adroit and dexterious machinery of government which is able to adjust itself to any situation and clothe it with a veil of justice and right, and which provides the tool to make the 435,000,000 colored people of the British Empire its utterly voiceless subjects; and which in addition has had virtually complete control of the government and commerce of China for over one hundred years, and of other apparently independent countries; so that it can reasonably be stated that over half of all the people of the world have been its subjects up to recent times. Of this government the late President Jordan of Stanford University said: "Everything runs as though newly oiled, and the British public hears nothing of it."

The manipulations of the financial oligarchy at the Berlin Convention to modify the Treaty of San Stefano had enraged many of the people of Europe and there followed some serious racial riots in Germany and Russia. The coming war in China against the financial oligarchy would very likely have been quickly followed by an uprising in India, with the whole British Empire subject to a searching investigation of the entire Concert of Europe, in which the British would have had only the very weak French support. However, the great depression of the 90's provided a solution, with the whole world in the grip of over-production and lack of markets.

It appears that about 1895 the first of the series of secret treaties between Japan and Britain, which made Japan virtually a British robot, was made. The British financial oligarchy practically took over the Japanese banking system to finance her wars and the immense industrial expansion which eventually swamped the world with goods made in Japan. Of this deal, the former Kaiser Wilhelm II wrote in his "Memoirs" published in 1921: "Some day when Hongkong has gone the same way, England will repent of her act. . . When once Japan has made a reality out of her watchword 'Asia for the Asiatics' and brought China and India under her sway, England will cast her eyes about in vain search of Germany and the German fleet."

France had now recovered from the beating of 1871, and the oligarchy was ready to lay the groundwork for a new world-wide balance of power, to supersede the noxious supervision of the Concert of Europe. By the treaties that followed on January 30, 1902 and in 1905, Japan became as close and subservient an ally of Britain as was France; and this alliance continued for about 35 years until it was ended by the assassination of the Japanese statesmen associated with the international financial oligarchy.

The thought that this Frankenstein of the financial oligarchy would eventually turn against its creators was expressed by Prof. Usher in his "Pan-Americanism" published in 1915, in these words: "Nor should it be forgotten that the financial indebtedness of Japan, which taxes the capacity of that country to meet the interest and principal payments, is all owed in Europe and America. So far as any tangible evidence of that capital is in existence in the world, it is in Japan. . . The Japanese have only to repudiate their entire indebtedness to free the nation from a staggering load and put it at once in the possession of its whole economic development at the price of what they have already paid. The control of the Pacific, the annexation of the Spice Islands and the Philippines, the expulsion of foreigners, the assurance for all time of financial independence—these are indeed things to conjure with. And we who can clearly see so much at so great a distance with so little aid, may well pause to wonder how much more the Japanese themselves can see, and how long caution and prudence will counsel them to wait before attempting the attainment of such desirable ends."

The oligarchy sent its Chinese henchman, Li Hung-Chang, on a tour of the European capitals to negotiate a Chinese concession to each of the Great Powers to allay the rising resentment of these powers in 1896, and to meet the coming Chinese Nationalist revolt. Each concession carried with it the requirement to help keep order in China. In this deal Russia was leased Port Arthur by the famous Li Hung-Chang-Lobanov Treaty of May, 1896, and subsequent agreements of September 8, 1896 and March 27, 1898. Germany was leased Kaiochow March 5, 1898, and Italy and Austria-Hungary also were given certain rights. The imminent Chinese revolt against the British yoke was represented to the people of the world as an indication of the extreme inner weakness of the Chinese dynasty and as an indication that China was on the point of falling apart in national disintegration, and that it was at the stage where the only solution was a division between the Great Powers.

That the weakness of the Chinese dynasty was not as great as represented may be apparent from the fact that the Emperor Kwang-Hsu ventured to dismiss the British hireling Li Hung-Chang with the support of the Nationalists in the summer of 1898, but as a result was himself deposed by the British, and Li Hung-Chang restored to influence under the nominal regency of the Empress Dowager. There are few instances in all history where there was more dissembly and falsification and feinting on the part of the Powers to keep the facts from the world as they were all implicated.

The American political machine of 1896 was faced with the difficult task of pulling the United States out of the great depression of the 90's and to fulfill their promise of "The Full Dinner Pail." The task was difficult, for in the words of Chauncey Depew, great financial and political power of that day, we were producing two thousand millions of dollars more goods than we could consume, and this overproduction was going back to stagnation and poverty. In this critical period a deal was struck by which the American Wall Street became a branch office of the Bank of England. (See footnote.)

The United States started its war with Spain ostensibly to free Cuba from Spanish oppression. Spain had fully accepted an American ultimatum on April 10, 1898, but this fact was ignored by President McKinley in asking for a declaration of war on the following day. On April 25, 1898, war was declared as existing since April 21st. The fleet of Admiral Dewey had been prepared for battle at Hongkong, and after receiving word of the declaration of war on April 27th, sped to Manila and attacked and sank the Spanish

---

Prof. Usher stated in "Pan-Germanism" of 1913, Chapter X, pages 139 and 140; that an understanding was reached, probably before the summer of 1897, that in case of war the United States would promptly declare in favor of England and France and would do her utmost to assist them; and that there seems to be no doubt whatever that no papers of any sort were signed. He quotes further: "The alliance, for it was nothing less, was based upon infinitely firmer ground than written words and sheets of parchment . . ."

fleet there on the morning of May 1, 1898. The American people were electrified by this unexpected and dazzling victory, and the resulting jubilation served to bury some questionable aspects.

Within the next few days the warships of various other Powers began to arrive at Manila, and there assembled a German fleet under Vice-Admiral von Diederichs and a British fleet under senior Captain Chichester. Admiral von Diederichs questioned the American action, which was his prerogative according to the then still tacitly accepted International agreements or International Law as promulgated by the Concert of Europe. It was the established right of every Great Power to be explicitly informed of any contemplated political change in any part of the earth, and to be given ample time to enter its objections and counter-proposals in every disagreement between any other nations, before any nation made any aggressive move.

The German fleet included some large and powerful armored ships and was superior to that of Admiral Dewey. Furthermore, the German Navy of this period was larger than that of America, as were also the navies of France and Russia. Despite this, Admiral Dewey assumed a highly bellicose attitude and in one exchange is said to have stated to Lieutenant von Hintze (later a foreign minister of Germany): ". . . and say to Admiral von Diederichs that if he wants a fight he can have it now." The reply of the British commander Chichester is said to have been equally to the point: "There are only two persons who know what my instructions are. One of those persons is myself, and the other is Admiral Dewey."

Various writers and historians differ as to the precise words used by Admiral Dewey, and they were "off the record;" but there is no question that Admiral Dewey used the fact he was addressing Admiral von Diederichs through a third person to use terms such as had heretofore been considered inadmissible in the intercourse between representatives of nations. The dispute at Manila raged on for three months and on August 13, 1898, the day after the war had ended and before word reached Manila, Captain Chichester is recorded to have placed his ships between the German and American fleets. The Germans then withdrew from Manila fully aware that the established law and order of the Concert of Europe had been superseded by "The New Order of Freedom" of a now fully revealed British-French-American-Jap alliance, and that their commerce and trade in the Pacific was on the wane.

Nicholas Murray Butler stated in an address delivered Sept. 1, 1940, at the Parrish Memorial Art Museum, Southampton, Long Island: "Consider for a moment the progress which was making from 1898 to 1920 in the building of a system of world organization and international co-operation that should control and guide the new economic forces which the Industrial Revolution had set at work. The purpose, of course, was to increase pros-

31

perity for all peoples, great and small, and to protect the foundations of international peace through international co-operation. . . Immediately, the progressive and liberal forces of the world rallied to respond to that appeal. . . It was the influence of the American delegation which gave to the first Hague Conference of 1899 the measure of success it attained. . . "The Spanish-American War in 1898 was absolutely unnecessary, and if it had not been insisted upon by the belligerent press, aided by numerous influential leaders of opinion, including Theodore Roosevelt, Cuba would have become free without any armed hostilities whatsoever. The cost to the people of the United States of that unnecessary war is quite appalling, since highly organized and efficient lobbies have provided for a system of pensions to persons whose relation to the war was only nominal, which have already amounted to tens of millions of dollars and will continue yet for a long generation. Isolation is the last thing of which the American government and the American people can be accused. . . "It is therefore obvious and of record that the American people were betrayed by the failure of those who were chosen to public office in 1920." (It is interesting to recollect that the Spanish-American War, whose eventual cost is here admitted as appalling, lasted a little over 3½ months.)

The condemnation of the Spanish American War and of the part played in its making by Theodore Roosevelt and others by Dr. Nicholas Murray Butler is a typical example of an imperialist deprecating imperialism, of the pot calling the kettle black; and there are few wars that have not been later deplored as having been utterly futile and unnecessary by some one of eminent standing whose connection with the International Imperialists was as positive as is that of Dr. Butler, the eminent chief of the Pilgrim's secret society of International finance. It all seems part of the general scheme to create confusion and contradiction in the minds of the people and so avoid disclosure of the highly disciplined organization of the international financial oligarchy and its planned objective of eventual world domination.

In "My Memories of Eighty Years," published 1924, Chauncey M. Depew records on page 270 a conversation in which Lord Rothschild offered Porto Rico and the Philippine Islands to the United States and stated the willingness of the Spanish Government to give independence to Cuba and to comply with every demand the United States can make. Regretfully he records further: "The proposition unfortunately came too late, and Mr. McKinley could not stop the war. It was well known in Washington that he was exceedingly averse to hostilities and believed the difficulties could be satisfactorily settled by diplomacy, but the people were aroused to such an extent that they were determined not only to free Cuba but to punish those who were oppressing the Cubans."

The facts are that McKinley suppressed Spain's formal acceptance of

American demands and asked for war the day after receiving that acceptance, and that it took every resource of high finance and its controlled jingo press to rush America into war before any resistance could be organized to oppose the war-makers. Mr. Depew guilelessly admits his significant conversation with Lord Nathan Rothschild over 25 years later when it apparently no longer has any current interest, and then this renowned after–dinner story teller and revered Pilgrim founder goes on to repeat the fable of why our war with Spain which is now accepted American "History."

Of how "History" is made, John K. Turner states in "Shall It Be Again," published 1922; "Remember that for more than four years one side was permitted to speak and the other forced to remain silent. 'The perspective that only time can give,' some say, 'is necessary before the true history of our war can be written, and before proper criticism can be made.' But the end of the fighting saw a vast and complicated machine feverishly at work to crystallize into 'history' the story of the war as it was told to us as propaganda in the heat thereof . . ."

Mr. Turner refers to the activities of another great Pilgrim at the conclusion of World War I on page 367: "Our illegal war in Russia was pleasing not only to Paris and London bankers, but to New York bankers as well . . . Mr. Lamont, a partner of Morgan was permitted to send an advance copy of the peace conditions to his Wall Street associates. While acting for the American people at Paris, Lamont participated in the organization of the China Consortium and the International Convention of Bankers on Mexico. So, along with the peace arrangements we find the beginnings of the "definite plan of international cooperation in the financing of foreign enterprises," advanced by Pres. Farrell of the U. S. Steel Corporation, a year before." (Note: It seems indisputable that this plan has been operating since 1897.)

VI

THE NEW ORDER OF FREEDOM

British approval of our entry into the new world Balance of Power was open and wide-spread; and the Right Hon. Joseph Chamberlain, Secretary of State for the British Colonies, made this comment on the secret pact between Britain and America: "We now see our cousins across the water entering the lists and sharing in a task which might have proved too heavy for us alone." The London Saturday Review quoted: "The American Commissioners at Paris are making this bargain, whether they realize it or not, under the protecting naval strength of England, and we shall expect a material quid pro quo for this assistance . . . we expect her assistance on the day, which is quickly approaching, when the future of China comes up for settlement . . ."

The pact between the British and American internationalists was made in the utmost secrecy, but many of the leading statesmen and educators of that day sensed what was going on, and many of the great speeches and articles in opposition to this fantastic conspiracy were included in "Republic or Empire?" by William Jennings Bryan, published in 1899; and among these is a speech delivered at the University of Michigan on February 22, 1899, by former Congressman Charles A. Towne, in which he said in part: ". . . upon the decision by the American people of problems now imminent depends the future weal or woe of our country, and hence that of the human race for ages to come . . . by a considerable portion of the public press the language of distrust of present tendencies is ridiculed as a form of hysteria or denounced as an attack on the Government, and that a man who ventures to raise a cry of warning is either charitably characterized as a fit candidate for a lunatic asylum or violently assailed as an enemy of his country . . . It is to mix up in alien quarrels, which we have deprecated always and with special emphasis of late, *at precisely the time when by all indications they are about to culminate in the most colossal and destructive war of modern times.*"

It would appear from the words of Mr. Towne that the treatment of "isolationists" has not changed in the 44 years that have passed; nor has British censorship and control over American sources of foreign news changed in the 65 years since Lieut. E. V. Greene commented on that control in his "Army Life in Russia" of 1878. (See footnote next page.)

Immediately after the nations of the world had been lined up in the "New Order," the long-awaited rebellion of the Chinese Nationalists broke out. The British organization to meet this menace functioned well and the cream of the British, French, Russian, German, Japanese, American, Italian and Austro-Hungarian armies soon gave the Chinese a severe beating for their aspirations of National freedom in what was known as the "Boxer War" of 1900. China was assessed an indemnity of $750,000,000 for her brutal aggression, later reduced due to American intercession and renunciation of her share. To impress upon the Chinese the utter dissolution of their national entity, the soldiers of all nations were marched through their "Forbidden City," thus desecrating their holy of holies.

With the other Great Powers of Europe locked up in the "policy of encirclement" on the continent of Europe by the overwhelming sea-power and imposing military and commercial over-balance of the new British Balance of Power, there was inaugurated an era of almost unrestricted territorial acquisition and plunder. The first was the attack and seizeur of the Orange Free State and the Transvaal Republic in the Boer War of 1899-1902, in the face of rather feeble and futile German protest; in which a mobilized British force of 448,435 eventually defeated 60,000 to 65,000 Boer soldiers.

The next move was to restore the status quo of China as the sole province of international finance, and with a nucleus of an overseas army released by the victory over the Boers to hold in check the reactions of the other European powers; the eviction of Russia from her warm port on the open Yellow Sea was inaugurated by the treaty of January 30, 1902 with Japan. The Japanese war machine was rapidly built up with British financing and in July of 1903

In "Barriers Down" published in 1942, Kent Cooper, General Manager of the Associated Press, discloses a 20 year battle fought since the end of World War I for the right to give the American people the truth about the news of Europe and the world, and he gives it as his opinion that the control of (page 7) "the greatest and the most powerful international monopoly of the 19th Century" in developing international atittudes and prejudices has been an undisclosed cause of wars for the past 100 years; that (page 264) the mischief planted during the fifteen years following World War I had become too great for the new relationship of the Associated Press to overcome.

He develops (page 106) that the determination of France and England to keep Germany encircled by small allied nations, was supported by Reuters and Havas with their own "cordon sanitaire." Havas, the allied French agency, is a subsidiary of the French Government; and an impressive array of practical and historical fact would indicate that most French governments of the past 100 years have been subsidiaries of the French House of Rothschild in practice if not in theory.

Mr. Cooper states (page 21) that the account is that international bankers under the lead of the House of Rothschild had acquired an interest in the three leading European agencies (Reuter, Wolff and Havas). Reuters, whose headquarters were in Old Jewry, near the Bank of England, in the City, was the chief of the three. It was the staggering presumption of this firm that the news of the world was its own private property, to be withheld, to be discolored to its own purposes, or to be sold to whom and where they directed. Rengo of Japan was obliged to pay a territorial "Franchise" fee, plus a service fee for news furnished. When Rengo attempted to buy news from the Associated Press; Reuters assessed a "service" fee on the Associated Press for the "right" to sell news to Rengo.

a demand was made on Russia to abandon her position on the Kwantung Peninsula. Russia had spent $300,000,000.00 in improvements since she had leased Port Arthur from Li Hung-Chang six years before, and the Jap challenge aroused a large measure of scorn in Russia, tempered only by the knowledge that this was a British challenge. (See footnote.)

There followed several months of inconclusive diplomatic interchange, and then, on the night of February 8, 1904, a Japanese torpedo flotilla sped into the harbor of Port Arthur, and with the Russian warships brightly illuminated and off guard, and with a large part of the crews on shore; inflicted terrific damage, sinking two battleships and a large cruiser. Many will recall the immense jubilation of the controlled American jingo press at this brilliant Japanese feat, and many of those of middle-age should still have a vivid recollection of the overwhelming wave of pro-Japanese sentiment that swept this country.

The Japs then transported nearly one-half million men over one thousand miles of open water and fought the two most massive engagements of modern times within eight months of the outbreak of the war, the battles of Liao-Yang and Mukden; the latter involving about 750,000 men and casualties of 130,000 men in less than a week. The Russians outnumbered the Japs, but were utterly crushed in a campaign of marvelous military efficiency, under the command of Field Marshal Oyama. The Jap ally had justified himself, and there was entered into immediately a new treaty in August 1905, signed concurrently with the signing of the Treaty of Peace between Japan and Russia, which bound Britain and Japan to immediately come to the assistance of each other, even if only one power was to attack. In the secret parts of this treaty there was undoubtedly included the removal of Germany from Kiaochow in the coming and planned World War I, and the award to Japan of the islands of the German Marianas, Caroline and Marshall groups stretching about 5000 miles east and west and 3000 miles north and south across our path to the Philippines; thus bracketing and nullifying our position in the Philippines,

---

When John Hay, in a characteristic assumption of sanctimonious hypocricy, remonstrated with the Russian Minister at Washington in May, 1903, stating that the inevitable result of the policy of aggression being pursued by Russia would be the dismemberment of China, Count Cassini shouted: "This is already done. China is dismembered and we are entitled to our share."

Norman Dwight Harris in "Europe and the East," published 1926, significantly states of British and Japanese co-operation in the affairs of Korea after the Sino-Japanese or Yellow War of 1895, that the Korean finances were re-established through Sir McLeavy Brown, a gifted British financial expert.

Already in 1900, with the Chinese revolution just in satisfactory solution by joint action of the Great Powers; the notorious international promoter of armaments, Basil Zaharoff, went to Japan to make a deal by which Rothschild controlled Vickers acquired armament and munitions plants in Japan with that prescient foresight of war profits ahead which marked the career of this man of whom Lord Beaverbrook said: "The destinies of nations were his sport; the movement of armies and the affairs of government his special delight. In the wake of war this mysterious figure moved over tortured Europe."

projecting the Japanese sphere of influence 5000 miles closer to our shores and making the Pacific a Japanese lake. The existence of this secret deal giving Japan these islands did not become known to America until Wilson sat down at the Peace Table at the end of World War I, and his objections to the various secret treaties that then came to light caused most of the secret deals to be revoked by the British, but this deal was not revoked.

The affairs of the Far East were now stablilized; in the opinion of some Englishmen for one hundred years to come; and all eyes turned to the new district of dissension in Africa. On April 8, 1904, a secret treaty was signed between Britain and France stabilizing the relative positions of these nations in Africa; in plainer words, dividing Africa between themselves. Trouble immediately centered in nearby Morocco, an independent empire which was occupied by the French in accord with the treaty with Britain. Germany promptly protested the French action as a breach of the Madrid Convention of 1880, signed by 15 nations, which had defined the precise status of Morocco; and then to offset and meet the breach of this Convention had herself occupied the port of Casablanca. (See footnote.)

From "A Short History of English Liberalism" by W. Lyon Blease published 1913 in England, Chapter XI re Liberalism Since 1906: "In 1904 Lord Lansdowne made an agreement with France by which the two contracting Powers settled all their outstanding disputes. This was intended by its author to be only the first of a series of international agreements. It was converted by Sir Edward Grey into a weapon of offence against Germany, the country upon which . . . the animosity of modern Toryism had definitely settled. The fortunes of Great Britain were bound up with those of France. The theory of the Balance of Power was revived, every diplomatic conference was made a conflict between France and Great Britain on the one side and Germany on the other, and in 1911 the lives and the wealth of the British people were endangered, not to maintain any moral principle or any British interest, but to promote the material interests of French financiers in Morocco. (page 364.)

"When Germany proposed at a Hague Conference, that international agreement should abolish the system of destroying private property at sea, Great Britain refused even to discuss the point . . . The right to destroy her commerce was our most powerful weapon against her, and as our peace policy was determined by our war policy, we preserved this relic of barbarism. The inevitable consequence of our diplomacy was to give German Jingoism an irresistible argument for the increase of the German Fleet. The increase in the German Fleet was described in threatening language by Mr. Churchill, and was matched by an increase in our own . . . There may have been information in the possession of the Foreign Office which justified this persistent hostility towards Germany. That country may have been animated by some desire to destroy our commerce, or to appropriate our Colonies. So far as we are allowed by our governors to learn any facts at all, there is no more than a shadow of a foundation for such a nassumption. Up to the end of 1912 we were bound straight for a conflict, of which not one Englishman in ten thousand knew anything definite, and not one in a thousand knew anything at all. (page 365.) (Note that this was written before World War I, published in 1913.)

"It is not the business of Great Britain to dictate to established Governments, or to go to war with them for the better regulation of their internal affairs. Nor is it the business of a British Government to refuse to make agreements with any foreign Government for the management of matters in which they are jointly concerned. But it is the duty of a British Government not to corrupt its own people by involving itself intimately with a Government whose methods are not only different but are utterly alien from its own. An

In order to arrive at an amicable settlement, a conference of the Powers was called at Algeciras, lasting from January 16th to March 31st, 1906. The British-French oligarchy passed the initiative at Algeciras to President Theodore Roosevelt, who through Ambassador White informed Germany in harsh and unequivocal terms to get out of Casablanca, that America would not tolerate any German port on the Atlantic. Thus the pact of the Pacific was extended to the Atlantic and our partnership in the British Balance of Power asserted in no uncertain terms. America forced virtually complete recognition of French pretentions and of the division of Africa between Britain and France. The financial oligarchy purchased Italy's vote at this conference against her German ally, by awarding Tripoli, then a Turkish province, to Italy; and promising British aid in its capture.

It is an interesting coincidence that Theodore Roosevelt proposed the nomination of John Hays Hammond for vice-president of the United States on the Republican ticket of 1908. Mr. Hammond was one of the four men sentenced to death in 1896 as a result of the Jameson Raid in South Africa, an effort to seize territory for the British Empire. Cecil Rhodes paid an indemnity of $250,000.00 to free Hammond and his brother, Col. Francis Rhodes.

With the African difficulties settled (perhaps for one hundred years) the scene flashed to the "Middle-East." Russia, balked in her efforts to attain a foothold on open water in the Near-East and in the Far-East, was now attempting to penetrate to the Persian Gulf. She had gradually occupied the northern half of Persia, while Britain had occupied most of the southern half to resist her, with a small neutral zone between. In order to meet the Russian menace, the British-French oligarchy decided to subsidize a certain section of the Russian Government, and a loan was arranged in April, 1906, of which a British writer(*) said: "The part played by the Foreign Office in advising the City is not easy to ascertain, but no one can doubt that our financial magnates were perfectly conscious of co-operating with the Foreign Office when they undertook to lend money to the Russian Government." The purpose of the loan was to strengthen the hand of those elements in the Russian Government favorable to International Finance, and to halt a growing tendency to an understanding with Germany.

---

alliance with France is bad only in so far as it is turned into a combination against Germany. An alliance with Russia is in itself unnatural and horrible." (page 367.)

These words written in 1913 by a Liberal Britisher about Britain apply with surprising exactness to the extent of the understanding and knowledge of the average American citizen as to why the United States is at war 30 years later.

(*)Bertrand Russell in "Justice in War-Time" (p. 168), published by The Open Court Publ. Co. in 1917.

The same British writer goes on to say: ". . . incidentally, we could not but help the Russian Government in suppressing the Duma, in reconquering Poland, and in depriving the Finns of the liberties which the Tsar had sworn to defend. . ." As a result of the British subsidy, the first Duma, whose probable pro-German leanings were greatly feared, lasted only ten weeks from May 9 to June 22, 1906. Although the Russian Emperor apparently was not in accord with this suppression of Russian liberty, its consequences eventually cost his life. Nor did the Anglo-Russian Agreement of August 31, 1907, made on the basis of the loans of the British and French bankers, end Russian pressure.

In November, 1910, Russia and Germany concluded the Potsdam Agreement, giving Russia a free hand in Persia. The same British writer states of this: "From this time on, we became completely subservient to Russia in Persia, since we lived in terror of a rapprochement between the Tsar and the Kaiser." As usual the public was totally unaware of the wider scope of the power politics involved and accepted the stock tale of Persia taken over by the two adjacent powers due to discord in Persia itself.

The British took a peculiarly artful advantage of the public ignorance in America in this instance in having the new British controlled government of Persia (the Shah and his government had fled to Russia) appeal to the American Government to assist it in regenerating the finances of Persia, and so help it to restore order and restore the independence of Persia. The success of this superficially plausible and highly commendable undertaking would of course have meant complete and final defeat of the last Russian hope for access to open water, the dream of centuries.

Russian antagonism to this splendid and humane objective was then thoroughly capitalized and exploited with the aid of alleged American financial experts, causing wide-spread indignation in America. The British-French loans to Russia had at this time reached vast proportions, as indicated by subject matter from the "Pan-Germanism" of Prof. Usher quoted heretofore; and this, together with the storm of American hostility, raised the weight of the Russians allied with the International Financiers so as to cause Russia to recede from her stand; giving to British diplomacy another mighty victory in the policy of encirclement. (See footnote.)

The foundation for The Great War, which had been started on May 1, 1898, was now nearly ready. Germany had made many other frantic efforts

---

Of the part played by Britain in the conflict of 1907-1912 with Russia which followed their agreement of August 31, 1907, to divide Persia between themselves, and which added much to the misery and poverty of the people of Persia, Mr. Arthur Bullard stated in an article which appeared in the Century Magazine for December, 1915, on "The British Foreign Policy and Sir Edward Grey": "From a humanitarian point of view the British record in Persia is the blackest in recent history. It is on a par with their Chinese opium war and their ultimatum to Portugal in 1790."

to evade the iron circle slowly closing about her national existence. The most outstanding was her effort to overcome a large part of British supremacy on sea by by-passing the Suez Canal with a railroad in Turkey to the Persian Gulf, the so-called Berlin to Bagdad Railroad. Although permission to build this line had been obtained from Turkey in the fall of 1899, shortly after the nullification of the Concert of Europe by the new British Balance of Power, she had been halted again and again by threat of war, and had not finished it by the outbreak of war in 1914.

The Berlin to Bagdad Railroad in general involved only an extension of about nine hundred miles to existing railroads, it was located entirely in Turkey and was being built with the full consent of that country. In the fifteen years from 1899 to 1914, the Balkans were called the sore spot of Europe, simply because of the jockeying with this railroad. The notorious agent provocateur of war, Sir Basil Zaharoff, was an active figure in the secret diplomacy of Europe in this period. One writer has said of this Greek-French super-salesman of the armament plants of International Finance, and British nobleman, that "His monument is the graves of millions; his epitaph, their dying groans." (See footnote.)

The principal reason for the frenzied secret diplomacy and bloodshed to halt this railroad was that it would have been a short-cut from Berlin to the East and India, by-passing the tollgate of the British-French financial oligarchy at Suez completely; with a considerable advantage over the route from London to India via the Suez Canal. Lord Cranbourne, Under-Secretary for Foreign Affairs, in January, 1902, stated that the maintenance of the status quo in the Persian Gulf was incompatible with the occupation by any Power of a port on those waters. British interests based their opposition on the fact that this railway would destroy the trade that English

---

Among the shadowy and mysterious figures that silently flitted about the stage of European power politics during the period of incubation (1895 to 1914) of the Great War, figures that all were imbued with that intense "passion for anonymity" generally associated with the great British-French banking dynasty, was Viscount Reginald Esher. Viscount Esher was born in 1852, the son of a noted jurist and interpreter of English law, and died in 1930. Despite the fact that he was for forty years one of the most powerful statesmen in all the world, his actual position was very obscure, and his name was utterly unknown and has remained unknown to the American public. In a hearing before the Committee on Foreign Relations of the United States Senate on January 28, 1940, it was developed that his whole position was derived from the fact that he was the most secret confidant and counsel of the "monarchy;" and it is quite apparent that by the term "monarchy" there is here meant the "King-in-Council" or Crown; or in other words the City and International Finance.

Harold J. Laski said of this man in the New Republic that he was "for a generation the unnamed member of Cabinet after Cabinet, indispensable to them all and not responsible to any." There was made a plausible arrangement to give a public aspect to his position of most secret confidant of the "monarchy" by his editing and arrangement of the letters and papers of Queen Victoria. In his Journals published in limited edition and entitled "The Captains and the Kings Depart" he recorded on August 3, 1917, as follows: "No American is likely to be killed before November. This is unfortunate, as Wilson may require to be steadied before then and only the death of young Americans can ensure him stability."

capital and English merchants had painfully built up along the Suez Route. An important aspect of this trade was the sale of coal to the ships of other nations at prices set by that English capital.

In order to provide a coaling station for her ships on the route to her own inner Africa colonies, Germany authorized a German syndicate to purchase dock facilities at Agadir, an utterly unimportant town on the southern end of the Moroccan Coast, with no railroad connection, cut off by mountains running out into the desert. This was not a political penetration as the town itself is cut off from all the world. Nevertheless, interference was set up; and when the German gunboat Panther was sent to investigate, it was forced out of the harbor by British and French cruisers standing by their guns ready to fire, in one of the most humiliating episodes of modern history. This incident in July, 1911, received wide attention as the "Morocco Affair," and was one of the last preludes to The Great War.

The outbreak of the Great War was fully expected by every government in the world; it took not one of them by surprise. The illusion which was artfully fostered in all the world that Britain was the victim of her treaty to defend Belgium neutrality, and of a wholly unexpected and brutal attack on Belgium, is evident from a sentence in a letter written to President Wilson by Colonel E. M. House, dated at London, May 29, 1914, in which he stated: "Whenever England consents, France and Russia will close in on Germany and Austria." The greater part of British sea-power from all over the world had been gathered in Home waters on that day; although Archduke Franz Ferdinand, active ruler of Austria-Hungary and leader of the foes of International Finance, was not assassinated until June 28, 1914; and war was not to start until August 1, 1914.

Sir Arthur Nicolson was for many years one of the foremost diplomats of the world. He retired in June, 1916, from the British Foreign Office. He can well be credited with a great part of the success of British diplomacy in restraining and confining the explosive economic pressure of the rapidly multiplying sixty millions of Germany squeezed in an area about four-fifths the size of the State of Texas; a pressure which erupted into World War I. Sir Arthur served for nearly a half-century in the Foreign Office and in nearly every important legation in Europe, the Near-East, the Middle–East and the Far-East.

While every other Great Power was represented by two delegates at the conference called at Algeciras in January, 1906, to consider the German protest against the Cambon-Lansdowne Agreement of April 8, 1904, which in effect had divided Africa and other parts of the world between Britain and France in utter disregard of existing agreements; Sir Arthur alone represented Great Britain and completely dominated the Conference. There was present only as an observer for British financial interests the Jewish Sir Donald

Mackenzie Wallace. Due to the intervention of Theodore Roosevelt, this partition of Africa was approved by the Conference, which ended in a complete diplomatic fiasco for the Germans, with even the delegation of their Italian ally against them due to previous secret concessions to the Italians in Africa by British Finance.

The tortuous currents and counter-currents of international machinations and intrigue over this period of nearly fifty years are described in intimate personal detail in "Portrait of a Diplomatist" by Harold Nicolson, a son of Sir Arthur, published in 1930. Mr. Nicolson states (Ch. XIV—The Outbreak of War—p. 298-299) in effect that the events of the several days immediately preceding the outbreak of World War I were merely of dramatic interest with no practical significance; that the war was the result of cumulative international stupidity since 1878. He further records (page 314) that his father wrote an article during that war expressing his indignation of the conclusion that Germany had started or was responsible for the war, an article which was refused publication. In that article, Sir Arthur Nicolson urgently warned that terms of oppression or humiliation of the defeated would make a durable or lasting peace impossible.

The following memorandum of a conference with President Wilson on December 10, 1918, was made by Dr. Isaiah Bowman, one of the American economic experts at the Peace Conference: ". . the President remarked that we would be the only disinterested people at the Peace Conference, and that the men whom we were about to deal with did not represent their own people. . . The President pointed out that this was the first conference in which decisions depended upon the opinion of mankind, not upon the previous determination and diplomatic schemes of the assembled representatives. With great earnestness he re-emphasized the point that unless the Conference was prepared to follow the opinions of mankind and to express the will of the people rather than that of their leaders at the Conference, we should soon be involved in another break-up of the world, and when such break-up came it would not be a war but a cataclysm. . ." (Vol. 4, p. 280, Intimate Papers of Col. House.)

Not only did those that "did not represent their own people" flout and nullify the views of President Wilson, but they also callously ignored the warning of their own foremost diplomat, Sir Arthur Nicolson, for many years the feared and formidable opponent of Germany in almost every major diplomatic clash, and the invariable victor due to the invisible support of International Finance; for Philip Snowden, later a member of a Liberal British Cabinet, said of the peace treaty: "The Treaty should satisfy brigands, imperialists, and militarists. It is a death-blow to the hopes of those who expected the end of the war to bring peace. It is not a peace treaty, but a declaration of another war. It is the betrayal of democracy and of the fallen in the war. The Treaty exposes the true aims of the Allies."

VII

THE NEW ORDER ENDS IN THE EAST

The common people of the world were kept in utter darkness as to the nature of the moves made in the great game of international power politics through the years, and the fact that it was a foregone conclusion that these moves would inevitably lead to gigantic slaughter, as forecast by former Congressman Towne in his speech of Feb. 22, 1899. Therefore, the outbreak of the Great War was to them a complete surprise, as it was also to the greater part of the representatives of the people in the government of the United States and in the government of the British Isles. The reasons given to the public for the war, were in general purely superficial and fraudulent. Belgium was a full British ally before she was invaded. The treaty as to Belgian neutrality which was alleged to have formed the basis for British intervention, was non-existent.

Specifically, the British foreign office pointed to a treaty signed April 19, 1839, as providing a basis for mandatory British intervention. It would take a considerable stretch of the imagination to read into the broad general terms of this treaty any such mandate. The British had in the meantime grossly violated far more definite terms of more recent treaties again and again, as witness the complete disregard of the 1880 Convention of Madrid signed by 15 nations, in their agreement of April 8, 1904, with France, dividing all Africa with France. It is very interesting to note the artless way in which the British Foreign Office admitted that its foreign policy of 1914 was still unchanged from that of 1839, in view of the rivers of blood shed in that foreign policy in the intervening 75 years.

The chicanery and deceit of international power politics was never better exposed than at the so-called "Peace Table" after the Great War. Herbert Hoover, who was a member of the American commission at Paris, tells of this in his article of November 8, 1941, in "The Saturday Evening Post," entitled "You May Be Sure I Shall Fight Shy." Mr. Wilson was stunned to find we had been fighting for the success of secret agreements of which the United States had no knowledge, some of them actually designed to check further political and commercial expansion of this country; such as that awarding the vast island chains in the Pacific to the Japs so as to cut us off from India, China and the Philippines. Italy had been promised a definitely described colonial area in another secret agreement for deserting her German and Austro-Hungarian allies; then later was blackjacked into the war with the threat to make peace and let her betrayed allies deal with her alone. (See footnote.)

This secret deal was retracted and Italy was given little for her 2,197,000 war casualties. The British Government seized nearly all of the captured areas for itself, taking 1,415,929 square miles and allowing France a mere 360,000 square miles for her immense casualties of 6,160,800 men(*). Italy was bankrupted and swept by revolution as a result, and out of this chaos emerged the inevitable dictator in the person of Benito Mussolini. Thus, was a powerful and faithful ally (and let those inclined to scoff contemplate the 680,000 Italian dead given to the British cause), transformed into a bitter enemy.

"The Intimate Papers of Col. House," arranged by Chas. Seymour, Provost and Sterling Professor of History, Yale University, and published in 1926 in four volumes, develop that a secret treaty covering Italy's reward for entering into World War I on the Allied side was finally formally signed at London on April 26, 1915, and was followed by Italy's declaration of war on Austria, May 23, 1915, and on Germany August 27, 1916.

From Mr. House's notes it would appear that this secret treaty, as well as one of March, 1915, promising Constantinople to Russia, were discussed at an intimate dinner meeting at the White House on April 30, 1917, attended only by himself, Mr. A. J. Balfour and Mr. Wilson. It seems that Mr. Balfour did not later furnish Mr. Wilson any particulars or details of the secret treaties as he had promised, so that Mr. Wilson testified before the Senate Foreign Relations Committee on August 19, 1919, that he had no knowledge of the existence of these secret treaties as a whole. ((Appendix, Vol. 3, p. 61.)

In the appendix on page 62 of vol. 3, occurs this statement: "There are those who believe the President laid too little stress upon the treaties and that he should have had some understanding with the Allies regarding them before he committed the United States to war." In vol. 3, page 322, is recorded a meeting with the President of which is stated: "The President was especially disturbed by the Treaty of London and the arrangements made for the partition of the Turkish Empire. Mr. Wilson was aware of the extent to which Britain and France were committed to Italy by the Treaty of London . . ." Strangely, this meeting occurred January 4, 1918; and in other parts of his notes he attempts to explain Mr. Wilson's forgetfulness in the matter of this treaty when he testified August 19, 1919, he knew nothing of these treaties as a whole.

On page 50 of Vol. 3, is recorded a copy of a letter dated Jan. 30, 1918, from Mr. A. J. Balfour to President Wilson, in which Mr. Balfour admits the secret treaties had been made by Britain under the stress of the necessity of getting Italy into the war, and expresses his doubt as to whether performance of Britain of her promises to Italy would be for the best interests of Italy. Thus was paved the way for the expulsion of Italy from the Peace Conference and the change from "The Big Four" to the big three, and eventually to "The Big One," Mr. David Lloyd-George.

Mr. House's record of a meeting with Walter Page, American Ambassador to Great Britain, on September 25, 1916, appears on page 319, Vol. 2, in part as follows: "He said the British resent our trying to bring about peace . . . I did not think this was as ignoble an effort as it seemed to Page. He declares none of us understand the situation or the high purposes of the British in this war. I replied that we resented some of the cant and hypocrisy indulged in by the British; for instance, as to Belgium. Page admitted that the British would have been found fighting with France even if France had violated Belgium in order to reach German territory more effectively . . .

From Vol. 3, page 41: ". . . neither the President nor House felt that it was possible to endanger unity with the Allies by raising a protest against the secret treaties."

(*) Ency. Brit.

In this atmosphere of corruption Mr. Wilson launched his proposed League of Nations as a successor to the former Concert of Europe in creating law and order among the nations of the world. In its original form, as proposed by Mr. Wilson, it reflected his idealism; but in its final form it was simply a fraudulent instrument to give a legal aspect to the control of the affairs of the world by International Finance.

In his "Memoirs of the Peace Conference" David Lloyd George stated that the prospect of a mandate for Armenia and Constantinople appealed to Wilson's idealism and he therefore made a proposal on May 14, 1919, to the Council of Four which was accepted by President Wilson "on behalf of the United States of America and subject to the consent of the Senate thereof."

Had the Senate succumbed to this crafty stratagem, it would have placed the United States at the focal point of infection of the wars of Europe, at the tangled crossroads of the centuries-old Russian surge towards open water and the German surge towards Bagdad, the Persian Gulf, the Orient and Africa. It would have simplified immensely the British problem of the Balance of Power, and made of the United States the immediate opponent of every European aggressor, and relieved the British Empire of this crushing load. Italy's dissatisfaction with the Peace Treaty, the seething ambitions of all the newly created buffer states to profit at the expense of each other, the war between Poland and Russia, the war between Greece and Turkey, the clash between Bolshevism and Fascism in the long and bloody Spanish War, and many more of the endless intrigues and hostilities that followed the Great War in the human cess-pool of Europe, would have involved the armed intervention of the United States at the expense of the American taxpayer.

This situation was sensed by American statesmen and the American public; and the proponents of this League of Nations and of the internationalist group on the Democratic ticket of 1920, Mr. Cox and Franklin Delano Roosevelt, were buried in a landslide so deep it seemed that the Internationalist control of America should have been buried forever. As a matter of fact a great number of people neither remember the names of the candidates on this Democratic ticket of 1920, nor the fact that Mr. Roosevelt made over 1000 speeches in favor of continued internationalist intervention in the campaign of 1920.

The election of 1920 removed America from the British Balance of Power, for the succeeding Republican administrations were true to their trust and mandate, and this country did not re-enter a British alliance until 1933. With the American withdrawal, history was repeating itself, for Britain was in the same situation that she had been in after France was demolished in the Franco-Prussian war of 1871. Where she had then come under the wing of the Concert of Europe for a number of years until France could recover and

Japan and America could be groomed as running mates, she now used the League of Nations for a number of years, until the newly formed buffer states reached a state of greater maturity under governments favored and supported by International Finance.

Poland grew to the status of a major ally, and in the formidable British-French-Polish bloc there were in addition Czecho-Slovakia, Jugo-Slavia, Greece, Belgium and Holland. Other countries, particularly Roumania, were for some years the battle-ground of opposing factions in the pressure to join this alliance. When Hitler and Franklin Delano Roosevelt came to power within a few hours of each other in 1933, the battle to submerge Germany again was under way. One of the early American contributions was the "Most Favored Nation" treaty, open to any and all nations in the world, except only Germany, then one of our best customers.

The peculiar ability of the arms and munitions makers to foresee war and to be all prepared and ready to make the profits is illustrated by an observation of H. C. Engelbrecht, Ph. D. and F. C. Hanighen in their "Merchants of Death" published in 1934: "Fifteen years have elapsed since the 'war to end all wars.' Yet the arms industry has moved forward with growing momentum as if the pacific resolutions of the various peoples and governments had never existed. All these technical improvements, all the international mergers, the co-operation between governments and the industry bear an uncomfortable resemblance to the situation during the epoch preceding 1914. Is this present situation necessarily a preparation for another world struggle and what, if any, are the solutions to these problems?"

Strangely significant, the great British industrial firm of Vickers, Ltd., in a major program of expansion with Rothschild financing, had entered the armaments and munitions field in the explosive year of 1897, at the very outset of the era of imperialistic expansion that brought on the Great War.

The eventual curious conjunction of apparently unrelated and widely separated acts in the world of politics and war seems to be well described in words used by Abraham Lincoln in commenting on a political conspiracy of his time: "when we see a lot of framed timbers, different portions of which we know have been gotten out at different times and places, and by different workmen . . . and when we see those timbers jointed together, and see they exactly make the frame of a house or a mill . . . in such a case we find it impossible not to believe that . . . . all understood one another from the beginning, and all worked upon a common plan, drawn up before the first blow was struck."

The Chinese Nationalists staged another of their periodical revolts against the British-French oligarchy and its Japanese ally in 1926, and as usual a number of Americans were killed in the general uprising against the foreign usurpers. A large force of Marines was sent to China under General Smedley

Butler to protect American interests. The British invited Admiral Clarence S. Williams, the commander of the Asiatic fleet to join them in shelling Nanking, the capital of the leader of the rebellion, General Chiang Kai-shek.* President Coolidge declined to permit the American fleet to join in this venture, thus bringing to the attention of the whole world that America was no longer a robot of the International clique, and causing one of the greatest upsets in the history of international power politics. Sumner Welles, a minor career diplomat during the Coolidge administration, attracted wide attention to himself by resigning in protest to the Coolidge foreign policy. Americans generally failed to grasp the significance of the outburst of hostility, insult and indignity to which American tourists were subjected in France and England directly after this incident.

Japanese writers had been bitterly indignant at a situation in which Japan had to fetch and carry at the bidding of the British-French financial oligarchy, had then invariably been obliged to turn over to them the fruits of victory, and been obliged to pay the oligarchy huge interest charges on the money to fight its wars. This open break in British-American relations placed the oligarchy completely at the mercy of the rebellious Jap factions; for, without American participation this situation in China lacked the essential flavor of democracy, left the oligarchy without sufficient forces to meet the rebellion, and opened them wide to the attack of their many internal British and French enemies.

The forces they had marshalled to again bring decency and democracy to China presented a somewhat dismal and moth-eaten aspect in comparison with the forces they had marshalled to subdue to Nationalist uprising of 1900. Then they had the assistance of the elite of the crack troops of America, Germany, Russia, Austria-Hungary, Italy, France and Japan to help them to subdue the brutal aggression of the Chinese. This time they made a shabby pretense that this was still a humane and unselfish effort to restore order in China and gathered together troops from what lands were still in their pay. They could only induce Portugal, Spain, Holland, France and Japan to answer their plea for help. They were obliged to sublet practically the entire job to Japan, and it was performed with the usual Jap snap and vigor. The consideration for the contract was an agreement giving Japan a wider participation in the commercial and political control of China, and conceding to Japan the occupation of Manchuria. (See footnote.)

(*) See "Old Gimlet Eye" (Smedley Butler) by Lowell Thomas, (p. 288) chapter on "Treading Softly in China."

From "Background of War" published 1937 by Editors of Fortune: "When the Lytton Committee made its report indicting Japan, and when China thereupon fought for the impositions of sanctions under Article XVI of the League, the British Foreign Secretary opposed the demand so eloquently and so effectively that the Japanese delegate, Mr. Matsuoka, told the American correspondents that Sir John Simon had said in half an hour

In order to minimize and discount their deal with Japan, enforced on them under the stress of circumstances, the financial oligarchy now subsidized its recent foe, General Chiang Kai-shek. They financed the Chinese aggression against Japanese occupation and infiltration, and thereby thoroughly enraged the Japs who felt that they had made an honorable deal and that they were now being double-crossed. International Finance had taken over the Japanese banking system under the treaty of 1902, and the great Japanese commercial expansion that then followed and which had flooded the world with Japanese goods, had been promoted by British capital. The wheels of the great Jap industrial machine slowed down with those of all the world, leaving the Japs with a huge interest load and rapidly falling revenue. This aggravated the very conditions which had been emphasized by Prof. Usher as a very probable cause for a Japanese war in his "Pan-Americanism" of 1915 in that excerpt quoted heretofore (page 29).

In this critical period the International clique was restored to power in the United States by the election of 1932, and the American Administration choose in giving the British unqualified support to ignore the fact that the position of the British interests in China had been dependent to a great extent upon Japanese support since the year 1895; that the Japs could have made common cause with the Chinese Nationalists or with Russia at various inopportune times, with a certain major disaster to the British Empire; that this was mainly a quarrel between Japan and the British interests as to Japan's share of the profits of the exploitation of China.

There was here a very close repetition of the plausible deal made in the case of Persia in 1911, when the British had ejected the Shah and set up a subsidized government of their own, then appealed to the American International clique to aid them in restoring control to the Persian Government, thus to balk the vital Russian surge to the sea by a simple strategy. In this instance, the secret control of China had been in British hands since 1841; so they utilized a revolutionist against their own secret government and made him the nominal front man, then appealed to the American International clique to aid them in restoring the government of China to its rightful head; thus to balk the deal they had made with Japan by a simple strategy.

That the British did not correctly evaluate their Jap ally at the beginning of their relations would appear from the ideology of Cecil Rhodes, cited

---

what he had been trying to tell the Assembly for weeks. From beginning to end of the Manchurian incident Great Britain resisted every effort to impose upon the aggressor country the penalties expressly provided by the League Covenant . . . the liberal British review, The New Statesman and Nation, charged ruling-class perfidy. "Behind Sir John Simon's pro-Japanese policy during the Manchurian dispute there lay the hope in the minds of businessmen, who were very adequately represented in the House of Commons, that Japan would fight Russia and repay our friendly encouragement in her piracy in China by a reasonable attitude when it came to dividing the spoils." (page 8-9.)

48

hereinafter; which was written at about the stage of the first alliance with Japan, and which embraces in the dawning British world state "the seaboard of China and Japan."

Chiang Kai-shek was forced to choose between two evils in going along with the British oligarchy after his defeat in 1927, but it is very obvious that he still has his Nationalistic aspirations, and that his open efforts to gain support in the United States for his dream of Chinese independence has caused a discordant note in his relations with the British. British dictatorship over American lend-lease has given him a very shabby deal. This latter fact was graphically treated in a recent book "Between Tears and Laughter" by the Chinese writer Lin Yutang.

VIII

THE LIBERALS VERSUS THE CONSERVATIVES AND WAR

The ebb and flow of British Imperialism and the predominance of the benign or the evil character of the Dr. Jekyll and Mr. Hyde British Government is definitely linked with the two major political parties of Britain as is readily apparent from the following tabulation of successive British Governments within present day personal recollection:

Period	Prime Minister	Party
1868	Benjamin Disraeli	Conservative (Tory)
1868-1874	William E. Gladstone	Liberal
1874-1880	Benjamin Disraeli	Conservative
1880-1885	William E. Gladstone	Liberal
1885-1886	Lord Salisbury	Conservative
1886	William E. Gladstone	Liberal
1886-1892	Lord Salisbury	Conservative
1892-1894	William E. Gladstone	Liberal
1894-1895	Earl of Rosebery	Pseudo-Liberal
1895-1906	Lord Salisbury et al	Conservative
1906-1916	A period of confusion	Unionists (incl. Conservatives)
1916-1922	D. Lloyd George	Coalition (Conservative majority)
1922-1923	A. Bonar Law	Conservative
1923-1924	Ramsay MacDonald	Liberal-Labor
1924-1929	Stanley Baldwin	Conservative
1929-1935	Ramsay MacDonald	Liberal-Labor
1935-1937	Stanley Baldwin	Conservative
1937-1940	Neville Chamberlain	Conservative
1940-	Winston Churchill	Conservative

For the purpose of ready identification the Conservative Party can be represented with the barbed tail, horns and cloven hoof of International Finance, intrigue and war; while the Liberals can be conceived to bear that torch of freedom and liberty usually associated in the public mind with England itself as compared to the other countries of Europe. That this aspect is substantially true becomes readily apparent in noting the trend of events under Liberal leadership and under Conservative leadership. Not only did the Conservative Benjamin Disraeli disestablish the Concert of Europe, but he deliberately led all Europe to the brink of war in the eastern question, after he had incited the ferocious Russo-Turk war of 1878.

50

When his ally Turkey was defeated and of no further use, Disraeli promptly inaugurated the subjugation and plunder of Egypt, vassal state of Turkey. The penetration was by the usual formula of partly fictitious loans to dishonest government and the building up of a heavy interest burden on the people. The subsidized Egyptian government was too weak in the face of the Nationalist revolution against this depredation of the public treasury, and the British-French oligarchy was then obliged to enter the civil war to protect their loans; thus inaugurating the long Egyptian war which was not settled for twenty years.

This brewing war upset the Disraeli government; and his Liberal successor, William E. Gladstone, greatest of all British statesmen, proceeded to withdraw from the Egyptian war. He commissioned the renowned agent of Imperialism, Gen. Chas. G. Gordon, to arrange for evacuation of British forces and British interests from the Egyptian Soudan. However, Gen. Gordon proceeded to act in complete contradiction to the prime minister's orders and in obvious accord with that ingenious dictum of Imperialism cited heretofore from the "Laws of England": "An executive or administrative act of a subject, though in the first instance done without authority of his Sovereign, will have all the effect of an Act of State if subsequently ratified." Thus had General Gordon met with success in his illegal venture, that success in itself would have upset the government opposed to it, and raised to power a government prepared to ratify it. Unfortunately, for General Gordon, he had climbed out far on a limb; and the Liberal Government, accustomed to this sort of trickery, simply left him in the lurch, with the result that he was killed in his venture; having vainly waited for months at Khartoum for succor.

In 75 years, from 1868 to 1943; in the entire span of life of our oldest living generation, there have been only two true Liberals to attain leadership of the British Government, William E. Gladstone and J. Ramsay MacDonald. During the period of 1906-1916, indicated in the foregoing tabulation as a period of ostensible confusion in national politics, the foreign power politics of Empire were not at all in a state of confusion; for, in that dexterious and chameleon-like ability to change its nature untrammeled and unhindered by any limitations of any Constitution, the foreign policy of Britain was centered not in any government, but was centered in the hands of only one man, Viscount Edward Grey, who became Secretary of State for Foreign Affairs in December, 1905, and retained that office for an incredible ten years until December, 1916, in a virtual dictatorship.

The views of Mr. William E. Gladstone, four times Prime Minister of Britain on a Liberal platform up to 1894, are very significant as he was the last Liberal Prime Minister before the Imperialist rampage that started in 1897 and continued up to World War I in 1914. The following quotations and notes are all from "The Life of William Ewart Gladstone", by John

51

Morley, published in 1903: "When England rejected the Berlin memorandum of May 13, 1876, in the Eastern Question which had been adopted by Russia, Austria, Germany, France and Italy—Gladstone said of Disraeli: 'His government is supposed now to stand mainly upon its recent foreign policy: the most selfish and least worthy I have ever known . . ." (Book VII, Ch. IV) A letter to the Duke of Argyll: '. . Dizzy's speech (so I call him with all due respect to the peerage), gave me a new light on his views. He is not quite such a Turk as I had thought. What he hates is Christian liberty and reconstruction. He supports old Turkey thinking that if vital improvements can be averted, it must break down; and his fleet is at Besika Bay, I feel pretty sure, to be ready to lay hold of Egypt as his share. So he may end as the Duke of Memphis yet.' Another letter to the same: 'I have a strong suspicion that Dizzy's crypto-Judaism has had to do with his policy. The Jews of the east bitterly hate the Christians.' Morley's note: Mr. G, however, found comfort in the thought that by the agitation two points had been gained: the re-establishment of the European Concert in the conference of Dec., 1876, and extrication from a disgraceful position of virtual complicity with Turkey. (See footnote.)

While Mr. Gladstone was definitely opposed to rapacious Imperialistic aggression and expansion, he was nevertheless an Imperialist. However, his imperialism was aimed at reconstructing and integrating and strengthening the existing empire, and he spent an immense amount of effort in attempting to arrive at a settlement in the dissatisfaction of the Irish; and had his lead been followed and had he been given full support, it is a reasonable assumption that Ireland would still be a full and loyal member of the British Commonwealth of Nations. He admitted that at one point in his career he had held with those favoring disintegration of the Empire. In 1872 he stated that opinion in the country was at last rising against disintegration. "In my judgment," he said, "no minister in this country will do his duty who neglects any opportunity of reconstructing as much as possible our colonial empire . . ." (Book VI, Chapter VIII.)

The Liberal government of Gladstone was followed by twenty years of

---

Although Mr. Disraeli had been baptized in the Church of England, he amazed and shocked one of his friends after coming out of a sitting in which he had defended the Church, by murmuring: "It is curious, Walpole, that you and I have just been voting for a defunct mythology . . ." His friend was further taken aback when Dizzy declared that there is no English nobility: "We owe the English peerage to three sources: the spoliation of the Church; the open and flagrant sale of its honours by the early Stuarts; and the borough-mongering of our own times. When Henry IV called his first Parliament, there were only twenty-nine temporal peers to be found. Of those twenty-nine only five remain." Then he explained that the only pedigree of long civilization was that of the House of Israel and that his family was far older than theirs. (Disraeli by Andre Maurois, Ch. IV) D. Appleton & Co. 1929.

Disraeli found pleasure in repeating a maxim of Cardinal de Retz: "Everything in the world has its decisive moment; the crowning achievement of a good conduct of life is to know and pick out that moment."

unbridled imperialistic aggression and expansion under unbroken Conservative control, ending in the gigantic slaughter of World War I with its total casualties of 37,494,186, and its 8,538,315 dead. These years of incubation for World War I (1897-1914) included the imperialistic aggression and seizure of the South African republics, the imperialistic "Boxer" war, the imperialistic Russo-Japanese War, the division of Africa to compensate France for British seizure of South Africa and Egypt, the Russo-British Persian imperialistic division, and the Balkan Wars in the interest of British Imperialism.

The mantle of dictator of the foreign policy of the Conservatives and of the British-French financial oligarchy, dropped by Sir Edward Grey in 1916, was assumed in large measure by Winston Churchill, whose start in high Conservative office occurred in 1903 in the reactionary Lord Salisbury government. In 1910, during the "Unionist-Conservative" period of 1906-1916, he rose to the office of Home Secretary, authoritatively stated to be the most powerful office in the British Empire, exercising the power of life and death in criminal cases; which under much vaunted English law are not subject to appeal, giving the powers-that-be a leverage against persons convicted of a political crime deemed possible by the uninformed only in the "Dictator" countries. (See footnote.)

He conducted certain secret negotiations usually associated with the Foreign Office, together with Lord Haldane, with Germany and Austria-Hungary in October, 1911, after he had just been made First Lord of the Admiralty. He arrived at certain very important decisions as to conduct of the Dardanelles campaign, and admitted full personal responsibility; having apparently conducted this campaign without approval or disapproval of his government. The Dardanelles debacle enforced a temporary interval in his positions of arbitrary power, but in June, 1919, he was made Minister for

---

From "Laws of England" Vol. 6, page 348, art. 499: To levy war against the King in his realm is treason, and this provision has been held to extend to cases of riot for various purposes. Thus a riot for the purpose of pulling down brothels or breaking open prisons has been held to be treason. And where riots took place in support of a prisoner undergoing trial, and Dissenting meeting-houses were pulled down, and other acts of violence committed, it was held to be treason. So also a riot in order to attain an object of a general or public nature, such as repeal of a law, through intimidation and violence, has been held to be treason . . . Note (m): Insurrections by force and violence to raise the price of wages, . . . or to redress grievances real or pretended, have all been held levying war."

Page 352, art. 508 — The punishment for a person convicted of treason is hanging. But the Sovereign may by warrant . . . , direct that, in place of hanging, the head of the convicted person shall be severed from his body whilst alive, and may also direct and order how the head and body are to be disposed of.

Except for the privilege of this singular choice in the manner of dispatching one convicted, the Sovereign appears to be fully as impotent as described in the words of Andrew Carnegie "in theory still a real monarch, although in reality only a convenient puppet, to be used by the cabinet (the City) at pleasure to suit their own ends;" not able even to exercise the power of pardon that is a prerogative of a governor of an American state and of the President of the United States.

War and Air. In this position he engaged in the persecution of the Irish which was made the subject of investigation by an American commission, which in its report charged that in this persecution and suppression the Irish had been subjected to indescribable brutalities and torture, and had been illegally deprived of their civil rights; and this report was a big factor in obtaining freedom for Ireland and in restoring a Liberal Government to Britain after a lapse of 29 years, in the person of Ramsay MacDonald. In 1935 the Conservatives were back in power and with them the period of incubation for the next world war was under way.

Few Americans comprehend the immensity of the British Empire, its land area just before this war nearly 17,000,000 square miles, not including the semi-colonial area of China; an area nearly six times greater than is the area of the United States itself. To the 1,415,929 square miles taken by Britain from Germany at the conclusion of World War I, there was added by purely Imperialistic aggression another incredible 1,145,764 square miles in the period from 1925 to 1938, years in which Americans generally were under the impression that everything was peaceful and quiet except for the belligerent and snarling dictators of Europe and the purges of Russia. Not only did Britain greedily seize 75% of the German colonies in utter disregard of the needs of her own allies and despite her already vast hegemony over a great part of the earth, but she was not prepared to stop there; the program of expansion was pressed year after year to the certain end that the over-populated areas of the world, deprived of any reasonable outlet for their products, would sooner or later rise in fury in a new and greater war. In 1939, the Germans seized about 100,000 square miles of Poland, but the British in that year seized 218,259 square miles in other parts of the earth.

Dividing the land ruled by the British Empire at this stage by the 49,000,000 population of the British Isles would give each Britisher a theoretical national interest in 120 times more land than had each German. Just before the war with Poland, Germany, greatest all-white nation on earth, had 104,133,000 people,* crowded into an area of less than 300,000 square miles. The entire British Empire had about 68,000,000 white people, ruling nearly 17,000,000 square miles of the earth's surface. We are now the victims of a grotesque and fanciful contention that the freedom and liberty of the United States is inextricably intertwined with the continued domination of these few Britishers over nearly one-third of the earth's surface; that our own safety is dependent on the protection extended over us by the illusive power of the great British Commonwealth of Nations; that our own mighty and compact and unified country with 135,000,000 people living in early the finest and most productive 3,022,387 square miles on earth, cannot continue

---
(*) 1939 population as per Whitakers British Almanac, 1941 — Eliminated from later issues.

to exist and to protect itself without the sheltering "umbrella" of the 68,000,000 white people of the British Empire scattered all over the face of the globe; their strength dispersed in the task of keeping the 435,000,000 colored subjects of the Crown under control.

As Winston Churchill ingenuously assured the American people: "Give us the tools and we will do the job (for you!)". That was in 1940, and the inspired press in that year was filled with the erudite discussions of pseudo military experts as to a forthcoming British invasion of Europe in 1941. The ways and words of International Finance are indeed wonderful.

The method and manner of British territorial growth and of British rule of their colored subjects is apparent from matter printed in the Congressional Record of March 4, 1941. From the New Leader, an organ of the Independent British Labor Party, the following is quoted: ". . . only a little more than a year ago the British Government annexed, by order in council, 100,000 square miles to the British Empire. This was done in February, 1937, in south Arabia. It was done in defiance of treaties of long standing. *It was done contrary to pledges solemnly given in the House of Commons*."

There was further given from The World Review, a British publication, an explanation by St. John Philby that the desire to acquire new oil fields led the British to commit this type of aggression, and he described the technique by which the job was done. He said: "That aerial bombing is freely used by the Aden administration is not denied by the Government. It is actually defended by those responsible for it, as a rapid and humane method of keeping peace in the outposts of the Empire." He developed further that the same method of keeping peace has been used by the Royal Air Force on many occasions along the northern border of India.

It is interesting to note that these methods of "pacification" were in use at least two years by the British before the Germans used them to "pacify" Poland and London.

Of the situation in India after the last war, Will Durant, in "The Case for India" published in 1930, states: "It was Woodrow Wilson who started the Indian Revolution. Did he know what he was doing when he scattered over every land his ringing phrases about democracy, self-government, and the rights of small nations? In every country — in Egypt and Near East, in China and India — there were ears waiting for those words as the signal to revolt . . . Were not the allies winning, and destroying the last autocracy in Europe? Was not the whole world now safe for democracy?" He further duscussed the brutal massacre of Amritsar on April 13, 1921, which touched off the Revolution of 1921, in which Brigadier General Dyer ordered his men to fire into a crowd of 10,000 Hindus "until all the ammunition the soldiers had with them was exhausted." General Dyer personally directed the firing towards the exits where the crowd was most dense: "the targets; he declared were 'good'." (p. 134). The massacre lasted over ten minutes. When it was over 1500 Hindus were left on the ground, 400 of them dead. Dyer forbade his soldiers to give any aid to the injured, and he ordered all Hindus off the streets for twenty-four hours, prevented relatives or friends from bringing even a cup of water to the wounded who were piled up on the field. It developed that these 10,000 people had entered an enclosure known as Jalianwala Bagh to celebrate a religious festival and the General had shot them all in the erronious view this was a political meeting. This did not feaze General Dyer and in the succeeding revolution the sadistic tortures inflicted upon hundreds of innocent victims exceeded those of medieval times (see page 135 of the above).

Is there anything significant in the fact that these Indian outrages were perpetrated under the direct jurisdiction of Minister of War and Air Winston Churchill? That the news of this reign of terror was kept from Parliament for six months? That General Dyer was presented with a cash award of $150,000.00 for his prompt and effective action despite wide–spread indignation in England?

Among the principles laid down by Woodrow Wilson for which the United States was alleged to be fighting in World War I, were the self-determination of suppressed minorities, the freedom of the seas, and open covenants openly arrived at. These were precisely the principles which International Finance was fighting against; but, if Woodrow Wilson presumed to enter the war on their side in the mistaken idea he was fighting for these things, they had no objection until the war was won. Then these principles were roughly over-ridden and cast aside by the leading allied statesmen in terms of open ridicule and contempt. Clemenceau called the Wilson "ideals" a joke on all humanity.

Again we are fighting the war of the Conservatives and of International Finance and of the City in the deluded pursuit of the very same idealistic objectives, resurrected and renovated and sweetened with the "Four Freedoms" and the "Charter of the Atlantic." Will these idealistic objectives be achieved with the winning of the war this time? Has the leopard changed his spots? In the words of one American (who has himself failed to do so): "Let's look at the record." Winston Churchill has been in many important respects the principal agent of Conservatism and of International Finance for nearly thirty years. He differs from his American collaborators in one distinct and definite respect—he does not sail under false colors. He has stated his position in clear and unequivocal words. He has stated that the "Four Freedoms" and "The Charter of the Atlantic" do not apply to "Those owing allegiance to the British Empire." He has further stated that the British Empire has been built by the sword and will be maintained by the sword.

The principles and purposes of the British Empire, the reasons for which it was conceived and for which were expended vast rivers of sweat and blood and tears in that process of building it by the sword, were laid down in these words by Benjamin Disraeli: "Gain and hold territories that possess the largest supplies of the basic raw materials. Establish naval bases around the world to control the sea and commerce lanes. Blockade and starve into submission any nation or group of nations that opposes this empire control program."

Winston Churchill, Conservative heir to the principles and methods of that greatest of empire builders and greatest of Conservatives, Benjamin Disraeli, stoutly affirms those principles and those methods of his illustrious predecessor. Mr. Gladstone stated: ". . I was tenaciously opposed by the governor and the deputy-governor of the Bank, who had seats in parliament, and I had the City for an antagonist on almost every occasion," (Mr. Gladstone and the Bank — Appendix Book 1 — Morley). That City, THE City, Citadel of International Finance, controls not only about half of the basic raw materials of all the earth directly, but also has an immense indirect influence over most of the rest of the basic raw materials of the world through its subservient financial interests.

Among the principal provisions outlined in the Atlantic Charter is that of access for all nations to essential raw materials and world trade for their economic prosperity, coupled with "Genuine Freedom of the Seas." The mines, the railroads, the utilities, the plantations, the raw materials, of South America, China, India, Africa, in fact practically of all the world, are controlled by the City. Who will determine what is a fair price at which the nations of the world are to have access to these sources of raw materials, ownership of which is in the hands of International Finance. That price was a big part of the argument which has brought on World War I and World War II. David Lloyd George stated in a speech at Plymouth on January 8, 1910: "We do most of the business of the world. We carry more international trade—probably ten times more—than Germany. Germany carries her own trade largely. The international trade is ours. Well, we do not do it for nothing. As a matter of fact, our shipping brings us over a hundred millions (pounds) a year, mostly paid by that wretched foreigner. I'm taxing the foreigner for all I know. . . You've heard a good deal of talk here, probably, about the exportation of capital abroad. There is no way in which we make the foreigner pay more. We get the foreigner in four ways by that. The first way we leave to Lord Rothschild . . ." (Better Times, published 1910).

It should be clear that this immense predominance in the business of the world and of the seas was not just due to a little British luck; that the control of the port facilities of the world, the British Navigation Acts, and other methods of restriction of the commerce of nations, backed by a fleet able to make them stick, was a potent factor. This predominance over the trade of the world is the life and the reason for the British Empire and Mr. Churchill is on record that there will be no change "incompatible with the status quo" of the British Empire.

In 1898, General J. B. Weaver stated in a speech: "The thing calculated to wound our pride in connection with the two speeches (by President McKinley and by the Right Hon. Joseph Chamberlain), is the fact that the Right Hon. Englishman spoke first and blazed the way in these recent discoveries concerning the ways of Providence with imperialism. Note the similarity of thought. It is marked and striking. It would seem there is an entente cordiale existing between the two governments which the people know nothing about."

It is quite evident there is again an entente cordiale existing between the two governments which the people know nothing about; an agreement in violation of any principle of open covenants openly arrived at; an agreement without sanction of the people of the United States or of their representatives in Congress. This would appear in part from a speech at Indianapolis by Secretary of the Navy Frank Knox on October 1, 1941, in which he stated that the "great peace-minded, justice-loving" powers—the United States and Great Britain—which are "lacking in any desire for personal aggrandizement" must join forces for at least 100 years to produce "by force if need be" an effective system of international law. He went on to say that the British and American navies "ARE sweeping the German pirates from the North Atlantic" and "eventually we shall lock Nazi Germany up in an iron ring, and within that ring of sea-power she shall perish." Here is a fairly good outline of a small part of that unquestionable secret agreement which accords with the course of events in the two years since that speech was made. Here is an open admission that we were already engaged in active combat over two months before the great surprise at Pearl Harbor. The previous flat statement of the Administration that it would not permit the British Empire to be defeated, that it was prepared to fight for the preservation of that Empire, added to events that have since occurred, indicate that this secret agreement is one making us a junior partner in the British Empire, the role lost by France.

The British Empire, whose ships have heretofore carried nearly 90% of American foreign trade through the years,* as well as that of other countires, could not exist if any other powerful nation was permitted "Genuine Freedom of the Seas" or unrestricted access to the world's sources of raw materials, except in the limited nature of a junior partner prepared to pay for partial participation in rivers of sweat and blood and tears. The only reservation originally made by the Allies in accepting Mr. Wilson's Fourteen Points, was complete liberty as to interpretation of the phrase "freedom of navigation upon the seas."

_____

(*) See World Almanac—various years.

IX

THE MONEY POWER IN POWER POLITICS

As developed herein from many aspects and from many authoritative sources, the functions of the British Parliament are restricted largely to the local and domestic affairs of Great Britain itself; and the parliaments of the four dominions of Canada, Australia, New Zealand and Union of South Africa are likewise confined to similar functions in their own countries. Thus, the 68,000,000 white people of the British Empire have forms of government which allow a nearly democratic form of administration of their own internal affairs, and this provides the stage-setting of Democracy behind which operates the secret "Sixth Great Power of Europe." The other 435,000,000 people of the Empire are subject to that provision of the laws of England which decrees: ". . Nor can the Crown, by proclamation or otherwise, make or unmake any law on its own authority apart from Parliament, except in colonies to which representative institutions have not been granted." (See the "Laws of England" by the Earl of Halsbury, Vol. 6, page 388, art. 582). (See footnote.)

The colored people of the British Empire, comprising 87% of the total population, are the voiceless subjects of the international financial oligarchy of "The City" in what is perhaps the most arbitrary and absolute form of government in the world. This international financial oligarchy uses the allegoric "Crown" as its symbol of power and has its headquarters in the ancient City of London, an area of 677 acres; which strangely in all the vast expanse of the 443,455 acres of Metropolitan London alone is not under the jurisdiction of the Metropolitan Police, but has its own private force of about 2,000 men, while its night population is under 9,000.

This tiny area of a little over one square mile has in it the giant Bank of England, a privately owned institution; which as is further elaborated hereinafter is not subject to regulation by the British Parliament, and is in effect a sovereign world power. Within the City are located also the Stock

---

From "Laws of England" Vol. 6, page 423, art. 651: In Crown colonies, namely, colonies to which representative, or representative and responsible government, has not been granted, the right of legislation enjoyed by the Crown is usually exercised either through a governor, commissioner assisted by legislative and executive councils nominated by the Crown or by the governor or commissioner, the Crown retaining the right of veto, and, in most cases, of legislating by Order in Council.

Exchange and many institutions of world-wide scope. The City carries on its business of local government with a fanciful display of pompous medieval ceremony and with its officers attired in grotesque ancient costumes. Its voting power is vested in secret guilds with names of long extinct crafts such as the Mercers, Grocers, Fishmongers, Skinners, Vintners, etc. All this trivial pomp and absurdity and horse-play seems to serve very well to blind the eyes of the public to the big things going on behind the scenes; for the late Vincent Cartwright Vickers, once Deputy-Lieutenant of this City, a director of the great British armament firm of Vickers, Ltd., and a director of the Bank of England from 1910 to 1919, in his "Economic Tribulation" published 1940, lays the wars of the world on the door-step of the City.

That the British people and the British Parliament have little to say in the foreign affairs of the British Empire, and that the people of the British Empire must fight when International Finance and the City blow the trumpet, appears from the paean of praise of America by Andrew Carnegie, "Triumphant Democracy," published in 1886 by that American super-industrialist and British newspaper publisher, in the following words: "My American readers may not be aware of the fact that, while in Britain an act of Parliament is necessary before works for a supply of water or a mile of railway can be constructed, six or seven men can plunge the nation into war, or, what is perhaps equally disastrous, commit it to entangling alliances without consulting Parliament at all. This is the most pernicious, palpable effect flowing from the monarchial theory, for these men do this in "the king's Name," who is in theory still a real monarch, although in reality only a convenient puppet, to be used by the cabinet at pleasure to suit their own ends." (Ch. XVI). (See footnote.)

In his damnation of Sir Edward Grey for the guilt for the Great War, entitled "Why We Are At War. A Reply To Sir Edward Grey," J. Ramsay

---

From "Laws of England", Vol. 6, page 427, Sec. 8, art. 658: "By the law of the English Constitution (nonexistent) the Crown acts as the delegate or representative of the nation in the conduct of foreign affairs, and what is done in such matters by the royal authority is the act of the whole nation, and binding, in general, upon the latter without further sanction ... The Crown, therefore, enjoys the sole right of appointing ambassadors, diplomatic agents, consuls and other officers, through whom intercourse with foreign nations is conducted, and of receiving those of foreign States, of making treaties, declaring peace and war, and generally conducting all foreign relations. Such matters are intrusted in general to the absolute discretion of the Sovereign, acting through the recognized constitutional channels upon the advice of the Cabinet or the Secretary of State for Foreign Affairs, unfettered by any direct supervision, parliamentary or otherwise."

Nicholas Murray Butler explained the nonexistence of a written British Constitution in a speech to the Pilgrims at New York on January 22, 1936, in these words: "Inasmuch as the Constitution of Great Britain is not fixed and definite, but is a matter of tradition and of habit, its interpretation is not by judicial voice but by legislative act. When, as in the Parliament Act of 1911 or as in the Statute of Westminster of 1931, a grave step is taken in changing the organization of the British Government, what they are really doing is amending their constitution thereby. That is why they do not have judicial interpretation of their Constitution, because not being written, not being definite, it can and must be dealt with as habit and necessity may require, ... "

MacDonald, later Prime-Minister of Britain and foe of International Finance, wrote in part: "It is a diplomatist's war, made by about a half dozen men."

There are on authentic record many instances where the City has acted not only without the consent of Parliament, but has acted in defiance of the wishes of Parliament and even in violation of its own solemn promises to the contrary of its action. From the "Laws of England" of the Earl of Halsbury it appears that the City, exercising its power as the "King-in-Council" or "Crown" has control over both the legislative and executive functions of the Empire, and as Britain has no written Constitution there is no court with any power to temper the actions of the "Crown." (See footnote).

Edwin J. Clapp, Professor of Economics at New York University, in his "Economic Aspects Of The War" published in 1915, developed the utterly boundless authority assumed by the "Crown" in its commands to the nations of the world through its "Order-in-Council," used without restraint and without reference to existing usage or so-called International law, by making new International Law to fit any situation, as required.

The Balance of Power is a creation of this financial oligarchy and its purposes are as follows:

(1) To divide the nations of Europe into two antagonistic camps of nearly equal military weight, so as to retain for Britain itself the power to sway a decision either way.

(2) To make the leading and potentially most dangerous military power the particular prey of British suppression and to have the second strongest power on the other side. To subsidize the "Most Favored Nations" with financial investments, and to permit them to acquire political ad-

---

The "Laws of England" by the Earl of Halsbury, recurrent Lord High Chancellor of Great Britain between the years 1885 and 1905, published in 1909, a massive work of over 30 huge volumes, states in Vol. 21, page 618, note k: "There is no rule of law which compels a Ministry which has lost the confidence of the House of Commons to resign office . . . In Vol. 6, page 388, art. 582: The *Crown* is therefore a necessary party to legislation, and neither House of Parliament, whether acting alone or in conjunction with the other House, has a power of legislation without the *Crown* . . . The *Sovereign* is regarded in law as being incapable of thinking wrong, or meaning to do an improper act. Apart from legislative authority, which is vested in Parliament *subject to certain concurrent rights of the Crown,* the law of the constitution clothes the person of the *Sovereign* with supreme Sovereignty and pre-eminence."

It is clear from the above that the representatives of the people in the House of Commons, and the House of Lords, are utterly lacking any legislative initiative and that their function in such matters *subject to certain concurrent rights of the Crown* is largely one of silent submission, and this is in accord with the conclusions of Prof. George Burton Adams. It clearly appears that while the Sovereign and the mythical Crown are not one, the virtues and authorities ostensibly vested in the person of the Sovereign pertain with full weight as to the Crown; and an act of the Crown is not subject to question in the Parliament, as the "King Can Do No Wrong." This provides the ideal machinery of government for the absolute rule of the Crown, and the world dictatorship of International Finance of The City; and the nature of this strange structure of government is further evident is this passage from the Encyclopedia Americana—Vol. 13 (Great Britain—English Judaism): ". . . the Crown, as chief partner in the Jewish money lending business . . . to secure its share of the gains . . ."

vantages under the beneficent protection of the Sea-Power, to the disadvantage and at the expense of the nations being suppressed.

(3) To subject the continent of Europe to the "Policy of Encirclement" so as to keep the nations of the continent in poverty and ineffectiveness, and thereby prevent the growth of sufficient commercial expansion and wealth to create a rival sea-power.

(4) To retain that complete control and hegemony over all the seas of the world, which was acquired by defeating the allied fleets of its only real rivals, France and Spain, in 1805; and which is artfully and subtly called "The Freedom of the Seas."

(5) To shift this Balance of Power as required so as to be able to strike down friend or foe in the rapidly shifting scene of world power politics, in that inexorable ideology that demands that everything and anything must be sacrificed where the future welfare and expansion to the eventual destiny of the Empire are affected; that eventual destiny outlined by its proponents as the eventual control of All the lands, and All the peoples, of All the world.

The ideology of the British Empire has been outlined in the past by various British statesmen and specifically by Mr. Disraeli (Lord Beaconsfield). The modern version which has been broadened to include the United States as a principal in the British Empire was outlined by Cecil Rhodes about 1895 as follows: "Establish a secret society in order to have the whole continent of South America, the Holy Land, the Valley of the Euphrates, the islands of Cyprus and Candia, the islands of the Pacific not heretofore possessed by Great Britain, the Malay Achipelago, the seaboard of China and Japan and, finally, the United States. In the end Great Britain is to establish a power so overwhelming that wars must cease and the Millenium be realized."

The secret societies of the above plan apparently came to life immediately after the death of Mr. Rhodes in the Pilgrims of Great Britain, often used by British statesmen in recent years as a public sounding board; and the Pilgrims of the United States, the latter founded in New York City on January 13, 1903, and listed in directories of secret societies with no indication of purpose. Mr. Rhodes left a fortune of about $150,000,000.00 to the Rhodes Foundation, apparently largely directed towards the eventual intent of his ideology. One admitted purpose was "in creating in American students an attachment to the country from which they originally sprang . . ."(*) It appears that organizations such as "Union Now," subversive to the liberty and the Constitution of the United States of America, have a large sprinkling of Rhodes scholars among their staff.

For some years there has been evident a gradually increasing tempo in

_____
(*) Encycl. Brit. "Cecil Rhodes."

the number and the degree of the attacks on the Constitution of the United States under guise of an inevitable drift towards union with the British Empire, and on August 20, 1941, Mr. Winston Churchill concluded this project had reached such momentum that he could afford to extend to it his blessing in these well-chosen words: "These two great organizations of the English-speaking democracies, the British Empire and the United States, will have to be somewhat mixed up together in some of their affairs for mutual and general advantage. For my part, looking out to the future, I do not view the process with any misgivings. I could not stop it if I wished. No one could stop it. Like the Mississippi it just keeps rolling along. Let it roll. Let it roll on in full flood, inexorable, irresistible, benignant, to broader lands and better days."

The guileless implication of something spontaneous, magnificent and overwhelming in this movement can be caustically exposed by referring to an autographed copy of "Pilgrim Partners" by Sir Harry Brittain, published in very limited edition in 1942. The sub-title of the book is "Forty Years of British-American Fellowship" and one critic stated in a review of the same: "The Pilgrims, founded in 1902, with one section in England, and one in America, was described some time ago by a leading New York paper as 'probably the most distinguished international organization in the world.' Each incoming American or British Ambassador receives his initial welcome from The Pilgrims, and gives his first address to the peoples of Britain or America respectively from a Pilgrim's gathering."

On page 113, Sir Harry records (and the capitals are his): "AT LENGTH, IN APRIL, 1917, DAWNED A WONDROUS DAY in Anglo-American history—the U.S.A. had jointed the Allies. The Pilgrims' dream of fifteen years at length had come to pass . . (page 115). A few days later a solemn service was held at St. Paul's Cathedral to mark the entry of the United States into the war, and the members of The Pilgrim's Club were allotted a place of honor under the dome, behind the King and Queen . . ."

The Pilgrims were founded in London July 24, 1902, four months after the death of Cecil Rhodes who had outlined an ideology of a secret society to work towards eventual British rule of all the world, and who had made particular provisions in his will designed to bring the United States among the countries "possessed by Great Britain." The first officers were Field-Marshal Lord Roberts, President; General Lord Grenfell, Chauncey Depew, and Captain Hedworth Lambton, Vice-Presidents; and Sir Harry Brittain as secretary. The representative committee elected included Mr. Don M. Dickinson of Detroit, Colonel Herrick of Cleveland and Charles T. Yerkes. The present American officers are listed as Dr. Nicholas Murray Butler, President; Major Elihu Church, Secretary; and Mr. Thomas W. Lamont, Chairman of the Executive Committee.

Sir Harry records that he was requested to come to New York in 1915 by the Chairman of the American Pilgrims "in order to give him a hand" in welcoming Lord Reading (Rufus Isaacs). The dinner in honor of Lord Reading took place at Sherry's on October 1st, and was attended by 400 representative men prominent in the banking, commercial and political life of the United States. In Sir Harry's words "dear old Joseph Choate" (former ambassador to Great Britain) presided.

The magic number of 400, once the symbol of reigning wealth and privilege, appears here in a new role. Men of millions here sway the destiny, the life or death of their fellow citizens, with an organization which is subversive to the spirit and the letter of the Constitution of the United States, an organization of which not one in one thousand of their fellow citizens has ever heard. The purpose of these men is completely interwoven with the dependence of their own invariably great fortunes on the operations of "The City," citadel of International Finance. Not only do these men collectively exert a planned influence of immense weight in utter secrecy, but they operate with the support of the immense funds provided by Cecil Rhodes and Andrew Carnegie.

The late Robert M. La Follette, Sr., in the course of a speech in the United States Senate in March, 1908, asserted that fewer than one hundred men control the great business interests of the country. His statement brought forth a nation-wide storm of denunciation and ridicule, and even today any similar statement is invariably derided as sensationalism and as "crackpot." Nevertheless, Senator La Follette conclusively demonstrated a few days later from the Directory of Directors that through interlocking directorates actually less than one dozen men controlled the business of the country, that in the last analysis the houses of Rockefeller and Morgan were the real business kings of America; and on Dec. 13, 1911, Mr. George M. Reynolds of the Continental and Commerical Bank of Chicago, stated to an exclusive company of bankers: "I believe the money power now lies in the hands of a dozen men. I plead guilty to being one, in the last analysis, of those men."

That the Rockefeller-Morgan-Aldrich machine, which was largely in control of business and politics then, is still a potent factor over a generation later, should be evident from the manipulations in the presidential election of 1940, charged to Thomas W. Lamont, president of J. P. Morgan & Co., and others; which has been made the subject of a Senate investigation.

Simon Haxey in "England's Money Lords Tory M. P.," published 1939, demonstrates in extensive tabulations that the peculiar inter-relationship and organization of the Money-Power in Britain places its control in a very few hands, and he quotes Mr. Hobson, who said: "Those who have felt surprise at the total disregard or open contempt displayed by the aristocracy and plutocracy of this land for infringements of the liberties of the subject and for abrogation of constitutional rights and usages have not taken sufficiently into account the steady influx of this poison of irresponsible autocracy from our 'unfree, intolerant, aggressive' Empire. (page 114.)

"What part do the Colonial peoples play in the battle for democracy, when they themselves have no democratic rights and the British governing class refuses to grant such rights? The pretended defence of democracy by the British Conservative Party can only be regarded by the Colonial peoples as a monstrous piece of hypocrisy. If Britain under a Conservative Government gets into difficulties, we can be quite sure that the Colonial peoples will refuse to help us, and wherever they feel strong enough, will seize power from the British governing class. The whole Empire is becoming tremendously unstable, and any great shock is certain to put an end to a situation where the business men of one small island rule over a great part of the world." (Page 115.)

The late Vincent Cartwright Vickers stated: ". . . financiers in reality took upon themselves, perhaps not the responsibility, but certainly the power, of controlling the markets of the world and therefore the numerous relationships between one nation and another, involving international friendships or mistrusts . . . Loans to foreign countries are organized and arranged by the City of London with no thought whatsoever of the nation's welfare but solely in order to increase indebtedness, upon which the City thrives and grows rich . . . This national and mainly international dictatorship of money, which plays off one country against another and which, through ownership of a large portion of the Press, converts the advertisement of its own private opinion into a semblance of general public opinion, cannot for much longer be permitted to render Democratic Government a mere nickname. Today, we see through a glass darkly; for there is so much which 'it would not be in the public interest to divulge' . . ."

The bulwark of the British financial oligarchy lies in its ageless and self-perpetuating nature, its long-range planning and prescience, its facility to outwait and break the patience of its opponents. The transient and temporal statesmen of Europe and particularly of Britain itself, who have attempted to curb this monstrosity, have all been defeated by their limited tenure of confidence. Obliged to show action and results in a too short span of years, they have been outwitted and outwaited, deluged with irritants and difficulties; eventually obliged to temporize and retreat. There are few who have opposed them in Britain and America, without coming to a disgraceful end; but many, who served them well, have also profited well.

While the City, through its ruling power of the "Crown" and its all-powerful Bank of England, holds the purse-strings of the British Empire; the Parliament still holds the taxing power within the British Isles, and the disposition of the citizens of Great Britain. This accounts for the incredible delay of the British Empire in getting started in its wars, and there has not been the slightest indication that the situation at the beginning of this war, which did not permit the Empire to draft a citizen for service outside of his homeland has ever been changed. This same situation existed in the case of the citizens of Canada, Australia, and the Union of South Africa; with only New Zealanders subject to draft in the services of the British financial oligarchy.

Gladstone expressed his ire at the usurpation of the functions of government by the Bank and the City, and both J. Ramsay MacDonald and David Lloyd George opposed International Finance. David Lloyd George covered this situation with the greatest sarcasm in his "Better Times" published in 1910, presenting eighteen of his speeches delivered 1903 to 1910, and from "The Peers and Public Opinion" delivered on December 17, 1909, at Walworth, there is this gem: "Who clamored for these Dreadnoughts? I remember a great meeting in the City presided over by Lord Rothschild, in which *he* demanded that there should be laid down eight Dreadnoughts. Well, we have ordered four, and *he* won't pay." He had stated previously at Limehouse in regard to this demand for more Dreadnoughts by the City: "That meeting ended up with a resolution promising that those who passed that resolution would give financial support to the Government . ."

David Lloyd George had been a red-hot radical, but made a complete about-face when he seized upon the Agadir crisis, which clearly foreshadowed the coming war in Europe, to spread out his wares before the bankers of the City in his speech of July 21, 1911, at the Mansion House in the City (and it was a deal). His career as a Liberal was doomed to an abrupt conclusion shortly in any event due to a dubious financial investment which he had entered together with his friend Sir Basil Zaharoff on the advice of the great Conservative Sir Rufus Isaacs, later war ambassador to the United States as Lord Reading; which caused an extensive scandal.

Eleutherios Venizelos, war-time premier of Greece; Georges Clemenceau and David Lloyd George were all known as the intimates and contact men of Sir Basil Zaharoff, and all went into eclipse in the Liberal uprising following the war (Encyc. Brit.—Zaharoff). David Lloyd George was obliged to resign in 1922 under a barrage of the British Liberal press demanding that Zaharoff be ousted from Downing Street.

In "Zaharoff, High Priest of War", published 1934, (page 276), Guiles Davenport uses the term 'systemé' to designate the rule of the City, and indicates that following World War I it had reached a new peak in its plan of world domination, able to remodel Europe almost at will, omnipresent and ominipotent in world politics.

X

THE SECRET SIXTH GREAT POWER

In "Germany and England" by J. A. Cramb, M. A., late Professor of Modern History, Queen's College, London, published in 1914, is quoted: "Napoleon in 1809 attempted to wrench a planet from the hideous tentacles of this octopus, this British dominion strangling a world . . . And what was the stake for which England fought in all her battles against Bonaparte? The stake was world-empire; and Napoleon knew it well . . . In the nineteenth century there was a long series of wars in all parts of the world—in the Crimea, in India and Afghanistan, in China, in New Zealand, in Egypt, in Western and in Southern Africa; so that it might be said without exaggeration that through all these years scarcely a sun set which did not look upon some Englishman's face dead in battle—dead for England. !"

The British had succeeded in destroying the preponderant French military might on the continent after 20 years of almost continuous turmoil and slaughter, in which almost every nation on the continent had been embroiled at one time or another; but British soldiers took little part in the fighting on the continent, even in the battles near the Channel commanded by the Duke of Wellington; for they were spread out all over the world engaged in seizing and occupying French and other colonial lands, and in fighting the United States in the war of 1812-1815.

While the "Battle of the Nations" at Leipzig, in which British forces took no part, marked the end of Napoleon's control over the European continent, he later escaped from Elba in the historic "100 days," and hurriedly organized a new army. He was overwhelmed in a four day battle on June 15th to 18th, 1815, in Belgium by an opposing force of 124,074 Prussians, 60,467 Hannoverians and other Germans, 29,214 Belgians and Dutch, and 31,253 British, who were largely raw recruits despite the fact that a 20 year British war was just being concluded. The Battle of Waterloo is generally accepted as perhaps the greatest and most glorious British victory of all time; but much British money and few British soldiers won the 20 year war with France into which Napoleon did not enter as dictator until Dec. 13, 1799, and the 31,253 largely inexperienced British soldiers did not single-handedly defeat the 124,588 hardened veterans of Napoleon near the village of Waterloo on June 18, 1815, and thus gain for Britain almost the sole glory for the defeat of Napoleon; while General Bluecher, the German victor at the gigantic slaughter at Leipzig, stood by in the role of spectator.

The House of Rothschild had its headquarters in Frankfort, Germany, and it had through its loans to the numerous small nations of continental Europe at extremely high interest rates, and in some instances of additional premiums, built up what was widely considered the world's greatest fortune, capitalized by general public custom as "The Fortune," previous to the war between England and France. Apparently foreseeing the trend of events, one of the sons of the founder was sent to England to open up a branch the year before Napoleon was elected one of the three consuls of France in 1799.

The financing of the war in France and the transmission of the funds to the troops on the continent was soon in the hands of this firm, and as this was a highly dangerous operation due to the presence of fast privateers, a high premium was paid for this service. Actually, the transfer was said to have been accomplished in part by signalling the French coast by semaphore or heliograph, or by ordering payment in writing in the modern manner from the continental branches of these bankers. The result of this was that the money paid in by Britain staid in Britain, while the funds on the continent were paid out, thus bodily transferring this continental banking house to Britain, with all its assets greatly enhanced by the transfer and removed into a haven safe from the grasp of greedy European statesmen and dictators.

When the conflict with France ended the House of Rothschild was in control of British finance and was the official banker of the British Government. This odd financial octopus was acknowledged to be in some respects the greatest power on earth and was designated by some writers as the "Sixth Great Power of Europe." Although the treaties of Europe and of the world were made under its dictation for 100 years, it never signed a treaty and it never was bound by a treaty. Its position was aptly described in the position of one of its agents and henchmen, Viscount Reginald Esher, as "indispensable to them all, not responsible to any." Despite the intense "passion for anonymity" of the Rothschilds, which has veiled their affairs in secrecy through the years; there are still a number of incidents of momentous international purport, some of them cited herein, in which their connection appears in an aspect denoting remarkable prerogative and ascendancy for what is only a private banking house.

While the gigantic fortune of Maier Amschel Bauer, who had lived once in a house bearing a red shield in Frankfort, Germany, had been a potent factor in the politics of Europe before the year 1800, the 1943 Encyclopedia Americana states under the subject heading "Rothschild:" "The political events of 1813 raised the House of Rothschild to the important position it has SINCE occupied in the commercial and financial world." And further: ". . . much intermarriage among cousins indicates *the family is destined long to retain control of European finance.*"

68

It was Nathan, founder the British house which plays so important a role in the affairs of the City and consequently in the affairs of all the world, who is credited with advancing this House to that commanding eminence of which Professor Usher stated in his Pan-Germanism of 1913: "Russia, Turkey, Egypt, India, China, Japan and South America are probably owned, so far as any nation can be owned in London or Paris. Payment of interest on these vast sums is secured by the pledging of the public revenues of these countries, and, in the case of the weaker nations, by the actual delivery of the perception into the hands of the agents of the English and French bankers. In addition, a very large share, if not the major part, of the stocks and industrial securities of the world are owned by those two nations and the policies of many of the world's enterprises dictated by their financial heads. *The world itself, in fact, pays them tribute; it actually rises in the morning to earn its living by utilizing their capital, and occupies its days in making the money to pay them interest, which is to make them still wealthier."* (p. 83)

In a carefully developed plan to attain financial control of all Europe, Maier Amschel established his five sons in the leading five financial centers of Europe; Nathan in London, Solomon in Vienna, Jacob in Paris, Karl in Naples, while the eldest (Anselm Maier) remained in the German headquarters. Nathan had arrived in England at a very auspicious moment in 1798, and he soon formed the depository for the vast fortune on the continent and its refuge from taxation; and the bloody struggle between France and England for world supremacy in what was actually modern World War I, which reduced all Europe into a vast sink of despair and bankruptcy; elevated the House of Rothschild to financial and political domination of all Europe and much of the rest of the world.

The Naples house ended about 1855 with the death of Karl; whose son, Maier Karl, moved to Frankfort to assume the German house of his childless uncle Anselm Maier, then 82 years old. After the death of Baron Maier Karl and his brother Wilhelm Karl, it was decided to abandon the sterile German headquarters; the cradle of the House of Rothschild. It is interesting to recollect the Disraeli observation that in effect holds that no country can be prosperous that does not offer prosperity to the Jews. Since 1895 the operations of the House of Rothschild and of the City have been very unfavorable to Germany throughout the world. The Vienna House ended with the Nazi occupation of Austria, and the Paris House moved to New York in 1940.

Maier Amschel laid down the maxims on his deathbed that all members of the family were always to act as one, that they choose wives out of their own family, that they must remain true to their orthodox religion. In accordance, his son Jacob (Baron James de Rothschild of Paris) married the daughter of another son, Baron Solomon of Vienna.

Nathan of London died in Frankfort in 1836 and was succeeded by his son Lionel, who married the daugher of Karl of Naples, his first cousin. Baron Lionel Rothschild died in 1879 and was succeeded by his son Nathan, who married his cousin Emma of Frankfort, and became the first Lord Rothschild in 1885. Nathan and his brothers, Leopold and Alfred, died during World War I; and the present head of the House of Rothschild is Lord Lionel Nathan de Rothschild, born 1882. The former head of the French House, Baron Edouard de Rothschild, born 1868, is a resident of New York City since 1940.

The Annual Encyclopedia of 1868 records that Jacob had been established in Paris in 1812 with a capital of $200,000.00 by Maier Amschel, and that at the time of his death in 1868, 56 years later, his fortune was estimated at over $300,000,000.00, and his yearly income at about $40,000,000.00. In comparison it may be significant to note that there was at this time no fortune in all America that equalled only one year's income of Jacob (Baron James de Rothschild). The fortune of the Rothschild family in 1913 was estimated at over two billion dollars.(*)

The biographers of the House of Rothschild record that men of influence and statesmen in almost every country of the world were in their pay. Some statesmen had the privilege of writing checks on the Rothschild bank at their own estimate of the value of their services. Disraeli was a very close friend of Lord Rothschild; and the extravagant Edward VII, acting King of England long before his mother died, was deep in their confidence. A large part of the profligate nobility of all Europe was deeply indebted to them.

Gradually through the years the House of Rothschild has withdrawn from the public consciousness and gaze in the practice of a peculiar "passion for anonymity" to the extent that a large part of the American public knows little of them and that they are generally considered in a class of myth or legend. It should be quite obvious that the gigantic fortune of this family is still a very formidable factor in the affairs of the world. The fact that the international loans to the nations of the world by Rothschild are still a live factor would appear from the many sharp barbs thrust at the omnipotent Lord Rothschild in the "Better Times" of David Lloyd George, and his further sardonic observation that Britain made some money on World War I. It is reasonable to suppose that the immensity of the Rothschild fortune has taken it more or less out of the scope of the present heads of the House of Rothschild and that it is merged in the general conduct of the financial, commercial and political control of the world by the City.

As recorded by their biographers, one of the most effective devices employed by the House of Rothschild through the years to destroy their competitors and to discipline recalcitrant statesmen has been that of artificially

---

(*) The Romance of the Rothschilds, Ignatius Balla, 1913.

creating an over-extended inflation by extended speculation, then to cash in and let others hold the bag. This trick was worked by them at intervals through the years. The Bank of England is in effect a sovereign world power, for this privately owned institution is not subject to regulation or control in the slightest degree by the British Parliament. A succinct outline of this situation appears in the Encyclopedia Americana under "Great Britain—Banking In." This privately owned and controlled institution functions as the great balance wheel of the credit of the world, able to expand or contract credit at will; and is subject only to the orders of the City, the City dominated by the fortune of the House of Rothschild and the policies of the House of Rothschild.

The fact that British capital played an important role in the great crash of the American market in 1929 seems beyond question. That the over-extended inflation that brought on the crash could have been controlled and halted dead at any point in its rise by the great balance wheel of the world's credit seems beyond question. That the immense crash and loss in American securities served not only to damage and cripple Britain's then greatest competitor, but also to discipline a recalcitrant and unfriendly administration seems beyond question. That $1,233,844,000.00 of foreign gold (*) was moved out of the country in the election year of 1932 to bring further discredit to that unfriendly administration and to influence the election seems beyond question. That $1,139,672,000.00 in foreign gold was moved into the country in 1935 to influence an election and to recreate "confidence" and to prepare the American investor for a further milking in 1937 seems beyond question. The fact that the House of Rothschild made its money in the great crashes of history and the great wars of history, the very periods when others lost their money, IS beyond question.

(*) World Almanac.

71

XI

A STUDY IN POWER

The giant oriental dynasty of the House of Sassoon, opium traders from Bagdad, became affiliated by intermarriages with both the French and English branches of the European colossus of international finance, the House of Rothschild; the first of which occurred in 1881. The House of Sassoon is now headed by Sir Victor Sassoon, a frequent visitor in the United States, who in recent years has urged "Union Now" in a newspaper interview in this country.

The history of this family is traced by Dr. Cecil Roth in "The Sassoon Dynasty," published in London in 1941. Already well-established financially, this family in 1832 broadened its sphere from Bagdad to Bombay; and thereafter into China, Japan and the entire orient. It recently had wide control over the financial affairs of the orient through David Sassoon & Co., Ltd., of China; the Imperial Bank of Persia; E. D. Sassoon & Co., Ltd., of India; E. D. Sassoon Banking Co. of China and London; Arnhold & Co., Ltd., of Shanghai, Hankow, Tientsin, Peking, Hong Kong, Canton, Mukden, London, New York, and other places; the Bank of China; the Eastern Bank; the British Burma Petroleum Co., and other firms. Captain Derek Barrington Fitzgerald, a Sassoon grandson, is recorded (page 222 of the above) as a considerable figure in "the City," financial capital of the world.

Li Hung-Chang, vice-roy of China until his death in November 1901, and agent of international finance, was reputed to be the richest man in China in his time; and was considered to be the owner of many great enterprises financed by foreign capital through the Sassoon owned Bank of China and Japan. This bank was organized in 1894, the year Japan attacked China in the Yellow War, to function in the new political and financial alliance between the British Empire and Japan which was inaugurated with this war. It was wound up in 1902, immediately after the death of Li Hung-Chang, and its interests were largely taken over by David Sassoon & Co.; which was reorganized into a limited company for this purpose in 1901.

With the "systemé" at an all-time high in its political power in 1920, Sir Philip Sassoon, Chairman of David Sassoon & Co., Ltd., was appointed Parliamentary Private Secretary to the Prime Minister, David Lloyd George.

Sir Philip, whose mother was Aline de Rothschild, went out of office with David Lloyd George in the political uprising in 1922 against the influence of Basil Zaharoff and international finance in Downing Street; and died in 1939.

Dr. Roth states (page 236) that "Lord Esher, sitting at the hub of the inner circle of English politics, wrote to him (Sir Philip) confidentially . . ." Dr. Roth also records a luncheon conversation at the home of Reuben Sassoon at which the composition of a Cabinet which Edward VII would find most nearly ideal was discussed, and it was suggested that "Lord Esher, of course, the power behind the scenes, would be the obvious Prime Minister." It is clearly indicated that the hub of British power politics was not considered to be in Downing Street, but that the Prime Minister was subject to the orders of "the power behind the scenes."

T. V. Soong, the present foreign minister of China, is also head of the Sassoon controlled Bank of China, which Mr. Elmer T. Clark describes in "The Chiangs of China," published in 1943, (page 71) as "ruling one of the world's great financial organizations." Mr. Soong is the son of a Chinese business man who was educated as a Methodist missionary in the United States, and was there babtized Charles Jones Soon. After returning to China in 1886, Mr. Soon changed his name to Soong. He wrote that his salary of $15.00 per month as a missionary was inadequate, and he therefore made a more profitable connection as a political agent of the Bank of China and Japan. His son, T. V. Soong, was educated at Harvard and was then given post-graduate training in an international banking house in New York. He was transferred to a Sassoon subsidiary in China about 1920.

Impressive historical record and authentic documentation reveal that the American kings of finance of the Rockefeller-Morgan machine entered into a secret agreement with the British-French-Dutch-Oriental combine in the early part of 1897 by which they regulated and allocated the business of the world among themselves much like the racketeers of recent years have split up the illicit liquor concessions in our big cities.

Their agreement was particularly designed to destroy the foreign commerce of Germany and of some other unfavored nations, and its operation necessarily demanded a concurrent secret military alliance, and this numbered among its ardent sponsors Theodore Roosevelt, then assistant secretary of the navy; Senator Henry Cabot Lodge; Senator Nelson W. Aldrich, widely reputed Rockefeller-Morgan associate; Chauncey M. Depew, known in some foreign countries as America's leading citizen; Rear Admiral Alfred T. Mahan, writer on power politics upon whom many foreign distinctions had been showered; and somewhat reluctantly, President William McKinley.

Japan was a member of this secret alliance through the House of Mitsiu, Rothschild-Vickers ally. There was a gradually rising dissatisfaction in

Japan through the years with her split of the international take, and in the early 1930's a rebellious military faction assassinated some of the officials and political associates of the House of Mitsiu, and thereby crashed a wide gap into the solid front of irresistable might with which the alleged justice-minded peace-loving powers had kept the brutal forces of aggression suppressed for over 35 years.

By its secret alliance, the United States was committed as a British-Jap ally to the Boxer War of 1900 in which foreign investments had to be protected against one of the periodical uprisings of the Chinese Nationalists; to the Russo-Jap War of 1904, settled by President Theodore Roosevelt for his ally in a master-stroke of diplomacy; to the Morocco Conflict of 1906 at Algeciras in which Theodore Roosevelt threw the full weight of American might into the scale to give Africa to his allies; and to World War I, where the language used by Theodore Roosevelt in denouncing the vacillation and delay of President Wilson exceeded the limits of ordinary decency.

Theodore Roosevelt was widely renowned in foreign lands as one of the foremost exponents of Machiavellian government of modern times, and few works on international politics through the years fail to accord considerable space to his many sly presumptions of power.

The death of Dr. Sun Yat-sen on March 12, 1925, left the foreign bankers without a moderating influence in Nationalistic circles, and the perennial war of the Nationalists with the bankers was promptly resumed in 1926. Their new leader, General Chiang Kai-shek, accompanied by the Soviet Russian General Michael Borodin, moved on Shanghai to loot the vaults of the foreign bankers. (The Chiangs of China, page 68.)

Then, in what was perhaps the most sensational upset in the history of international power politics, an incident widely condemned by internationalist writers as the direct cause of World War II, President Calvin Coolidge declined to honor the secret commitments of the United States and refused to permit American ships and troops to engage in active hostilities against the Chinese Nationalists.

In this extremity, the bankers sent Mr. T. V. Soong to negotiate with Chiang Kai-shek. He offered Chiang $3,000,000.00 in cash, his own pretty sister May-ling as a wife (Chiang already had a wife and family), and the presidency of China as successor to Mr. Soong's deceased brother-in-law Dr. Sun Yat-sen. Chiang accepted the offer and ordered his Russian allies to get out of China, and the wedding took place in December, 1927.

In 1940 Mr. T. V. Soong offered to hold off a Japanese attack on the United States until this country could prepare itself to meet the attack when it came for the sum of $100,000,000.00, which in effect was to be a flat gift to China. Mr. Ernest O. Hauser records in an article appearing in Life in

1941, that the President called in his financial manager, Jesse Jones, and that it was decided that "The merchandise was fantastically cheap at that price" and that this "bill of goods" was therefore "bought." It would seem that Mr. T. V. Soong, as head of the Bank of China, was selling a "bill of goods" for his principals of the House of Sassoon which has a striking resemblance to the "bill of goods" sold by Mr. Winston Churchill when he offered: "Give us the tools and we will do the job."

In the early 1900's, the House of Sassoon was at the peak of its power, and its members, who had all gradually drifted to London from the orient, entertained in lavish magnificence, and Dr. Roth records that King Edward VII was a very constant house guest and companion of its members, and that among other greats and future greats of these years partaking of their intimate hospitality were A. J. Balfour, H. G. Wells and the rising Winston Churchill.

Mr. H. G. Wells has been engaged through the years in distorting and falsifying international history in the service of the secret empire of finance. His "What is Coming? A European Forecast," published in 1916, was written to impel American entry into World War I, and its subject matter has been largely used to bring about American entry into World War II, with only minor transposition of names, as may be apparent from a few sentences, as follows:

". . . The Hohenzollern Imperialism towers like the black threat of a new Caesarism over all the world (p. 208). If by dying I could end the Hohenzollern Empire tomorrow I would gladly do it (p. 214) . . . The American tradition is based upon the casting off of a Germanic monarchy, it is its cardinal idea. These sturdy Republicans did not fling out the Hannoverians and their Hessian troops to prepare a path of glory for Potsdam (p. 222). . . For fifty years Germany has been unifying the minds of her people against the world. She has obsessed them with an evil ideal . . . (p. 223). This catastrophic war and its preparation have been their chief business for half a century . . . (p. 270). We fight dynastic ambition, national vanity, greed, and the fruits of fifty years of basely conceived and efficiently conducted education. (p. 272) . . . If Germany remains Hohenzollern after the war, to do their utmost to ring her in with commercial alliances, tariffs, navigation and exclusion laws that will keep her poor and powerless and out of mischief so long as her vice remains in her (p. 273)."

Charles A. and Mary R. Beard in their recent Basic History state (p. 442): "On the basis of clear documentary evidence scholars dissected the myth, propagated by those Powers, that Germany was wholly responsible for inaugurating the war . . . The gleaming mirage that pictured the World War as purely or even mainly a war for democracy and civilization dissolved beyond recognition . . ." The Beards merely recorded history, while Mr. Wells was merely selling a "bill of goods."

Over 400 years ago, the Florentine statesman Niccolo Machiavelli engaged in a profound study of methods used by various rulers to attain power. He lived in an age when nations were small, in some cases only walled cities, when events were moving fast and when many men were struggling for power. Due to his own confidential government position, he was able to observe events in other lands and in his own closely, he was able to evaluate the methods of those who succeeded and to observe the mistakes of those who failed. In "The Prince" he reduces his conclusions to definite rules or doctrines. His conclusions, in general, appear to find support in the De Monarchia of Dante written two hundred years before "The Prince."

The findings of Machiavelli and other students of power decree that to obtain power it is essential to ignore the moral laws of man and of God; that promises must be made only with the intention to deceive and to mislead others to sacrifice their own interests; that the most brutal atrocity must be committed as a matter of mere convenience; that friends or allies must be betrayed as matter of course as soon as they have served their purpose. But, it is also decreed that these atrocities must be kept hidden from the common people except only where they are of use to strike terror to the hearts of opponents; that there must be kept up a spurious aspect of benevolence and benefit for the greater number of the people, and even an aspect of humility to gain as much help as possible.

It is held that the vast mass of the people are oblivious and gullible, and therefore will believe a lie which is repeated again and again, regardless of how obvious may be the fundamental facts to the contrary. But, in Chapter VI of "The Prince" is decreed also: ". . . matters should be so ordered that when men no longer believe of their own accord, they may be compelled to believe by force."

Mr. Wells illustrated a practical application of the doctrines of power in his book of 1916, mentioned previously, in declaring that it was the resolve of sensible and influential Englishmen to beat Germany thoroughly and finally, and, if Germany remains Hohenzollern after the war, to do their utmost to ring her in with commerical alliances, tariffs, navigation and exclusion laws that would keep her poor and powerless and out of mischief so long as her vice remained in her.

Thus, Mr. Wells first hypocritically divulged part of the exact technique which had been in use for fifty years to exclude Germany and other unfavored nations from the colossal commercial dominions and monopolies of the private empires of the dynasties of finance, and then cunningly distorted the reality of the past and the present as a proposed future punishment.

This is an application of the doctrine of power which holds that high-minded words can be used by the powerful, the demogogue and the hypocrite, or the merely self-deluded, to arouse passion and prejudice and sentimentality for the wrong reasons in favor of disguised real aims; thus to deceive the people and to lead them by easy stages to sacrifice their own interests in the service of power.

It is obvious that in the early stages of the usurpation of power in any land of even partial democracy, opposition is certain to arise, and that an attempt to suppress this antagonism by arbitrary means would quickly inflame and solidify the opponents into an overwhelming attack. Machiavelli considered this aspect and indicated the correct method to neutralize this danger in stating: "Many consider, that a wise prince, when he has the opportunity, ought with craft to foster some animosity against himself, so that, having crushed it, his renown may rise higher."

This indicates the technique of modern Machiavellians in having their own stalking horses grasp the leadership of their opponents, and then as their own veiled and hidden action is gradually unfolded, have their Pied Pipers oppose them on spurious and superficial reasons in such a way as to obscure and conceal as far as possible the real reasons and objectives; thereby confusing and confounding the real opponents and leading them into a swamp of futility.

Since the Rothschild dynasty attained control of British finance 130 years ago, every major war has been fought to utter collapse of British opponents and unconditional surrender, and has left international finance omnipotent and unrestrained in organizing a new power-block to enforce the peace and to exploit the victory. Each of these successive power-blocks has failed in a brief length of time due to the desertion of an ally infuriated by the boundless greed of the British bankers, and has led to a new war, and these wars have been of progressively greater scope and fury.

Only France has been a constant ally for over a century, and the reason seems quite evident as the House of Rothschild has controlled both Britain and France during this period. In "Inside Europe," published in 1936, John Gunther develops (Ch. IX) that any French prime minister, at the end of 1935, was a creature of the financial oligarchy. That this financial oligarchy was dominated by twelve regents, of whom six were bankers, who were "hereditary regents" in the absolute sense of the term, and were headed by Baron Edouard de Rothschild.

War, according to Machiavelli, must be applied at almost regular intervals to maintain power. It is held that it is not an unforeseeable accident and that it is not a passing madness, but that it is a normal and indispensable tool of power. It must be applied promptly and ruthlessly to be effective in its function of maintaining and extending power.

The infinite danger of the present position of the United States in its relations with the all-pervading power and presumption of the allied dynasties and empires of finance, appears from the dogmatic assertion of David Lloyd George in his "Better Times:" "The international trade of the world is ours." The Machiavellian methods used in acquiring this power are admitted by Mr. Winston Churchill in his statement that the British Empire was built by the sword and will be maintained by the sword.

Machiavelli very urgently warned against any alliance with a more powerful friend, and counseled that in cases where this was unavoidable, the stronger friend must be regarded as a certain potential enemy who must be undermined and destroyed as soon as circumstances permit with the aid of the common enemy and of weaker friends.

The Machiavellian nature of the British Government appears from a consideration of British policy by Rear Admiral Charles L. Hussey in "The United States and Great Britain," published in 1932 for The Chicago Council on Foreign Relations by The University of Chicago Press, as follows (p. 171): "The British have no written policy, nor even a written constitution . . . To undertake to outline British policy, an American must be both capable and daring. It seems the part of wisdom to turn to the British themselves for this. The editor of a British colonial weekly tersely stated it as follows: 'Britain is the workshop of the world. It lives by foreign trade, therefore, to secure and hold markets it must invest money abroad, acquire colonies and *control the seas* . . . The world must be made safe, not for democracy — for that is only a word — but for trade and commerce. . . That is the national policy of the British people, of both Liberals and Conservatives. It forms the background of all British thinking. It is not openly stated, as there is a trace of Oriental secrecy and reticence in England. It is not considered good form to shout one's beliefs from the house-tops."

XII

THE PROBLEMS OF THE PEACE

The Rhodesian ideology was outlined in a letter written by Cecil Rhodes in the autumn of 1890 and made public by W. T. Stead in the Review of Reviews of May, 1902, immediately after the death of Rhodes, in part as follows: "What an awful thought it is that if we had not lost America, or if even now we could arrange with the present members of the United States Assembly and our House of Commons, *the Peace of the world is secure for all eternity*. We could well hold your federal parliament five years at Washington and five years at London. The only thing possible to carry this idea out is a secret one (society) gradually absorbing the wealth of the world to be devoted to such an object . . . I note with satisfaction that the committee appointed to inquire into the McKinley Tariff report that in certain articles our trade has fallen off 50 per cent, and yet the fools do not see that if they do not look out they will have England shut out and isolated with ninety millions to feed and capable internally of supporting about six millions. If they had statesmen they would at the present moment be commercially at war with the United States, and they would have boycotted the raw products of the United States until she came to her senses . . ." Mr. Stead further records in this same article that Mr. Rhodes worked with the support and backing of the Rothschild's in his mammoth undertakings and speculations in Africa.

When Mr. Rhodes considered the problem of "ninety millions to feed" he was looking a long way into the future, for the Great Britain of 1890 had a population of only 37,000,000 including Ireland. Like Mr. Depew, he felt the need of doing something very drastic about foreign markets and demanded an immediate boycott of the very nation with which he also wanted union in order to force down its tariffs, so British goods could undersell American goods in the American market. The vicious circle started by this foreign interference would as its next step have forced the reduction of American wages to the much lower British level to regain the market, and so on ad infinitum.

When we entered the alliance of 1897 with the British Empire in order to create an overwhelming British control of the Balance of Power, and agreed to assist the British Empire in the permanent encirclement and repression of Germany, Russia and China (with the latter requiring immediate, urgent and active attention), we adopted one of the two opposing theories of geopolitical thought referred to by Prof. Spykman in "America's Strategy in World Politics." The controlling factor towards this alliance was a wide acceptance of the Rhodesian ideology that with such an alliance, "the peace of the world is secure for all eternity." This fallacy has persisted practically up to the present in an utterly fatuous belief in the eternal omnipotence of British "sea-power."

The foreign trade statistics of the United States in the years since 1897 demonstrate very conclusively that the statement of Lord Salisbury in 1898: "The appearance of the American Republic among the factors, at all events, of Asiatic, and possibly of European diplomacy, is a grave and serious event, which may not conduce to the interests of peace, though I think, in any event, it is likely to conduce to the interests of Great Britain;" was far more to the point than was the fatuous eloquence of Chauncey M. Depew proclaiming in 1900 that "by the statesmanship of William McKinley . . . we have our market in the Philippines, and we stand in the presence of eight hundred millions of people, with the Pacific as an American lake . . ."

That the Pacific simply became much more of a British lake than it had been is very apparent by combining the totals of the foreign trade of the United States with those lands in the British colonial orbit whose exchange largely balances United Kingdom purchases, with the figures of the United Kingdom; in other words, adding together the foreign trade of China, India, Malaya, the Philippine Islands, and the United Kingdom. We then compare the years 1897 when we joined the "policy of encirclement" and the year 1927 when Mr. Coolidge definitely withdrew our support of the British alliance, at the time when it had become involved in the war with the Nationalists under Chiang Kai-shek.

Foreign Trade of the United States in Millions of Dollars (World Almanac):

Area or Country		1897	1927	Increase
The Orbit of British Finance	Sales to	$ 555	$1071	93%
(United Kingdom, China, India, Malaya, Philippine Islands)	Purchases	176	1035	488%
Germany (relatively smaller	Sales to	153	482	215%
and poorer in 1927)	Purchases	70	201	187%
Grand Total of U. S. Foreign	Sales to	1061	4865	363%
Trade with All Nations	Purchases	764	4185	448%

In 1927 a weak and improverished Germany still accounted for 41% of the narrowing favorable margin still remaining to the United States in its sales to all the nations of the world over its purchases. On the other hand the highly favorable margin of sales over purchases in our trade with the British orbit which existed in 1897 had almost disappeared in 1927. The year 1927 was in most respects the best year of the post-war era of prosperity preceding the great depression. Our sales to a defeated and smaller Germany in 1927 were over three times greater than they had been in 1897, while our sales to the British orbit, which had profited immensely from the imperialistic expansion of 1897-1920 and from further war and post-war expansion, did not even double; and actually contracted due to the much greater volume of post-war business activity and lesser purchasing power of money. However, we did very well by our British ally, for we bought six times more goods from the British orbit in 1927 than we did in 1897.

Our trade with Germany was about as important as our trade with all of Latin America. Germany was a heavy buyer of American raw materials and an American competitor in selling manufactured goods in Latin America. The Latin American countries, particularly those of South America, were competitors of the United States in selling raw materials to Germany, and were buyers of American manufactured goods. We competed with Germany in the Latin American market throughout modern times, and held our own very well, and the deadly menace of this competition to our continued national existence was not evident until it was given a promotional build-up for the world-wide boycott of German made goods inaugurated by the International Conference called at Amsterdam in the early part of 1933 in retribution for German misdeeds.

The United States promptly joined in this boycott with its "Most Favored Nations" treaties to which every country in the world, except only Germany, was eligible. This was not a step short of war; it was war, and it was sure to lead to eventual bloodshed. Had a boycott of this type been enforced against a relatively small and weak country like Cuba or Venezuela, it would have ended in open fighting. When German toys, dolls, cutlery, wines and other goods disappeared from the counters of American merchants (to be replaced by goods marked "Made in Japan"), the German market for American wheat, meat and cotton disappeared also; and there was invented the remedy of plowing under surplus crops and of killing off surplus little pigs.

When the American financial-political machine of 1897 decided that a very drastic expedient was necessary to forcibly acquire foreign markets to absorb the two thousand millions excess production over what we could consume, the population of the United States was about 76,000,000, and averaged about 25 per square mile of what is nearly the finest and most productive land on earth. When the American machine of 1933 decided upon a similar expedient for similar reasons, their principal opponent was a nation which according to late statistics has a population which averages 352 per square mile of a country containing almost as much mountainous and other unproductive area in proportion as the United States.

In attempting to evaluate the explosive and dynamic opposing forces in this situation, forces that threaten to destroy this civilization, Prof. Usher in his "Pan-Germanism" of 1913 states (page 247): "England, France, Russia,

81

and the United States already possess the choice places in the world; their position is already everything they could reasonably hope to have it; and they scarcely deserve to be praised for unselfishness when they insist upon preserving a situation which is so very much to their advantage . . . Nor is it proved that they have obtained it by the observance of the ethical precepts which they would now be glad to apply to Germany . . ." As to Germany's position he states (page 233): "If Germany is wrong, others too have been wrong; indeed, if her conduct is unjustifiable, no country in the world can establish its moral and ethical right to existence." It is noteworthy that since this was written in 1913, England and France improved their already dominant position immensely, largely at the expense of Germany; thus to aggravate the problem.

If an America with only 25 people per square mile and almost unlimited access to the good things of this earth was headed back into stagnation and poverty unless it could sell two thousand millions more than it could consume, and a Britain in control of one-third of the markets and the raw materials of all the earth was in such need of the markets of the American workman in America that the great high priest of "Union Now" would advocate commercial warfare against the United States in 1890 in order to force their surrender to Britain, where will all this end? The British scramble to forestall us in the markets of the world right now should be a fair indication of trouble ahead, not only in our foreign affairs but also at home when the American workman can no longer be kept employed by giving our surplus production away and charging it to the American taxpayer.

In following one of the two opposing theories of geopolitical thought and in the alleged purpose of retaining for the United States its foreign markets, more money has already been spent than the gross total of our sales to all the world in all the years of our existence; an expenditure that makes a mockery of what profit or capital may have been derived from this source, and makes a mockery of all proved economic thought. The fundamental facts are that nations do not trade with one another because they are political allies or political opponents. Foreign nations buy from the United States because they need what she has to sell and because they want to sell their own products in return.

The actual position of the United States in the power politics of the world was well outlined by Prof. Usher in "Pan-Germanism," Chapter X, pages 141 to 143: "The possibility of invasion (of the United States) is made of no consequence by the simple fact that no foreign nation possesses any inducement for attempting so eminently hazardous an enterprise. The United States possesses literally nothing which any foreign nation wants that force would be necessary to obtain, while, by making war upon the United States, she would certainly expose herself to annihilation at the hands of her enemies in Europe, who have patiently waited for decades in the hope that some one of them would commit so capital a blunder . . ." ". . . the complexity of the problems of no one group of states, whether in Europe, in the Middle East, or in the Far East, could possibly allow the United States to play a prominent part. In each, the natural antipathies counteract each other. Only the fact that every nation is anxious to maintain or win power or wealth in Europe and Africa and Asia *makes the United States of value to any of them.* Indeed, it is only as European questions become themselves factors in the larger problem of India, Morocco, and the Mediterranean that they concern the United States at all. As soon as European politics became world politics and Asiatic and African problems became European, the United States began to be a factor in their solution. *She has, to be sure, no vital stake in any one of these fields . . ."*

There have probably been over 100,000,000 casualties and over 25,000,000 dead in the wars of the European Balance of Power in the modern era, and as the greatest interval between major wars in this 130 year period has never been over 24 years and the minimum interval has only been 12 years, every generation—usually assumed to be about 33 years—has had one or two major wars, and this recurring slaughter has been the subject of much inconclusive and perplexed discussion. (See footnote.)

A monstrous structure of bigotry and intolerance has been artifically devised throughout the Christian world which dogmatically rejects any recognition of the fundamental disease underlying the recurring symptoms of war. Most of the political leaders of the United States have not been acquainted with the most elementary fundamentals of the two opposing theories of geopolitical thought, and in making these two opposing theories merely two sides of a debate have given vent to surprisingly simple-minded statements.

That many of the problems of the peace being discussed now still bear a striking resemblance to those confronting the world following the gigantic slaughter of the Napoleonic War, when the end of the war found the people of Europe stunned with horror, imploring their statesmen and rulers to find some solution of this recurring slaughter of innocent human beings, may be apparent from the following from "The War and Democracy" by J. Dover Wilson, published in London in 1918: "The Congress of the Powers which met at Vienna in 1814 to resettle the map of Europe, after the upheavals and wars of the previous twenty-five years, was a terrible disappointment; and we, who are now (in 1918) hopefully looking forward to a similar Congress

---

In "England's World Empire" by A. H. Granger, published in 1916, is given this statement by C. H. Norman: ". . . Nor is British Navalism innocuous in its spirit! Through that navalism, Britain has assailed nation after nation in Europe that has threatened her trade supremacy; and Germany, the latest comer, is being similarly handled. 'On the knee, you dog!' was a phrase that rang unpleasantly through England not long ago . . ."

at the end of the present war, cannot do better than to study the great failure of 1814, and take warning from it. The phrases which heralded the approaching Congress were curiously and disquietingly similar to those on the lips of our public men and journalists today (1918) when they speak of the "settlement" before us. "The Parliament of Man, the Federation of the World" . . . seemed in 1814 on the eve of accomplishment. The work of the Congress was to be no less than "the reconstruction of the moral order," "the regeneration of the political system of Europe," the establishment of "an enduring peace founded on a just redistribution of political forces," the institution of an effective and a permanent international tribuanal, the encouragement of the growth of representative institutions, and, last but not least, an arrangement between the Powers for a gradual and systematic disarmament . . . The Congress of Vienna was to inaugurate a New Era. (Pages 31-32.)

". . . the only man who at first voiced these aspirations of the world at large was the Russian Tsar, Alexander I., and such concessions to popular opinion as were made were due to what the English plenipotentiary, Lord Castlereagh, described as the 'sublime mysticism and nonsense' of the Emperor."

That history repeats itself, again and again, and again; may become apparent from the fact, that one hundred years later that eminent servant of International Finance, Georges Clemenceau, termed Woodrow Wilson's Fourteen Points and "the subsequent addresses" as a joke on history; and these Fourteen Points were completely washed out and eliminated before the end of the Peace Conference of 1919.

The British objectives in the Napoleonic War were stated in a few simple and forthright words in which the British Government declared that it was not its intent to fight the French people—only to rid Europe of the Scourge of Napoleon, bring peace to Europe and preserve the rights of small nations; and these same words, with a mere change of names, have served to explain the British position in all the succeeding wars of the Balance of Power, including World War I and World War II.

Unfortunately, the exigencies of power politics after every cyclical war have been such that it was invariably deemed expedient to sacrifice some small nations for the general good, and a typical example is cited by Ford Madox Hueffer in "When Blood is Their Argument," published in London in 1915: "I think the time has come when we may say that the one crime that this country (Britain) has committed against civilization was its senseless opposition to Napoleon. It was, to me, extraordinarily odd to hear the British Prime Minister the other day talk of the Campaign of 1815 as a war of Freedom. For, if you come to think of it, by the treaty after that war, Great Britain, the Holy Alliance and Metternich . . . affirmed upon Poland the triple yoke of Austria, Russia and Prussia . . ." There is a similar indictment by some British author of note on practically every war of the Balance of Power fought by Britain.

As to the fate of the working classes who fought the war with their blood and their life's savings in the case of a country which had achieved total victory after a long costly war, the Illustrated Universal History of 1878 records: "Great Britain emerged from the long contest with France with increased power and national glory. Her Empire was greatly extended in all parts of the world; her supremacy on the sea was undisputed; her wealth and commerce were increased . . . But with all this national prosperity, the lower classes of the English people were sunk in extreme wretchedness and poverty."

In "Old Diplomacy and New," 1923, the British writer A. L. Kennedy states: "There is more than a grain of truth in the witticism that "Conferences only succeed when their results are arranged beforehand'." When the Financial Commission at Genoa met to discuss the stabilization of currencies, 250 delegates forced their way into the room. A sub–Commission "No. 1" was formed for the transaction of the most important political business on which Germany was represented. But for ten days it was given no business to perform. The work was done in conversations between the principal Allied representatives meeting at Lloyd George's villa.

In his "Memoirs of the Peace Conference" Lloyd George records a memorandum which had been presented by him March 25, 1919, for the consideration of the Peace Conference: "You may strip Germany of her colonies, reduce her armaments to a mere police force and her navy to that of a fifty-rate power; all the same in the end if she feels that she has been unjustly treated in the peace of 1919 she will find means of exacting retribution from her conquerors." There is every indication that Lloyd-George considered the Peace Treaty as merely a temporary stop-gap to be renegotiated after ten or fifteen years because he made some contingent agreements of that length.

XIII

THE FIVE IDEOLOGIES OF SPACE AND POWER

By the tested and effective device of constant repetition the international claque has manufactured into apparently accepted fact the falsehood that the United States has heretofore had no established foreign policy. That this is not true may be apparent from a consideration of the five great ideologies involved in the modern struggle for space and power, listed in the order of their presumed geographical scope. They are as follows:

1. The secret ideology of international finance, which has been described in comprehensive and precise detail hereinbefore, and which is aimed at eventual rule over all the world by the British Government. World rule by a closely knit and well-disciplined group of special privilege, secret mostly only in the United States as most European people have a fair conception of its existence and workings.

2. The ideology of Russia which was originally conceived in the Will of Peter the Great. A. H. Granger in "England's World Empire," published 1916 (page 173) dwells on the fear of the Russian Pan-Slavic ideology which has overshadowed Europe for over a century, and he quotes the whole of this document which is directed at first eliminating the obstacle of Austria and Germany, then proposes the conquest of India and Persia, and ends with the words: ". . . which will ensure the subjugation of Europe." This fundamental scope has been broadened to encompass the entire world by the Bolshevist doctrine of world rule by the proletariat, with death to Capitalism and the International Capitalist."

3. The ideology of Japan "Asia for the Asiatics," with its pretentions to almost half of the people of the world in a confederation dominated by Japan.

4. Pan-Germanism, German political control over the European continent, freedom from British restriction of the seas, and "the open door" in the trade and commerce of all the world.

5. Pan-Americanism, prerogative of the United States of political control of the Americas; the ideology of "America for the Americans," given early expression by the Monroe Doctrine.

Not only was Ideology No. 5 the expression of the established foreign policy of the United States from 1823 to its abandonment 75 years later by the adherents of the ideology of world rule by international finance, in order to ally the United States with the wider scope of Ideology No. 1; but it is still the fundamental ideology of those in favor of that theory of geopolitical thought which proposes isolation from the entanglements of Europe and Asia. (See footnote.)

The first four of these ideologies all overlap and clash in their scope; and even the total destruction of any one would still leave a fair balance among the other three; which would restrain any one of them from exposing itself in an attack upon the Americas and the United States; particularly, if the United States could achieve real unity in the Americas. But the abandonment by the United States of its own ideology No. 5 to align itself with Ideology No. 1 with the avowed purpose of totally destroying Ideologies No. 3 and No. 4, will leave only the world embracing and absolutely opposed Ideologies No. 1 and No. 2 to possibly engage in a duel to the death with the aid of such subjugated peoples as each can wheedle or compel to join its forces. Such a duel seems inevitable in view of the deep animosities and the explosive economic pressures already existing.

That those in control of American foreign affairs do not propose to retain any allegiance to Ideology No. 5, or of making it an ideology within an ideology, and to evidently give the British Government assurance of this fact, seems indicated by the delegation of American purchases and of American finances in South America to British deputations and commissions. It would seem impossible as participants of Ideology No. 1 to maintain the iron tariff wall permitted us under the policy of isolation, which has been the principal bulwark of a scale of wages and a scale of life far above those of other countries; regardless of its condemnation at times due to misuse by selfish interests.

Of the five great ideologies of the world only the Pan-American ideology ever substantiallly attained its objectives. It is the oldest of these modern ideologies except for that part of the Russian ideology expressed in the Will of Peter the Great, and that part of Ideology No. 1 laid down early in the history of the British oligarchy in the following rules of empire:

1. Gain and hold territories that possess the largest supplies of the basic raw materials.

2. Establish naval bases around the world to control the sea and commerce lanes.

The expression of isolation by the Monroe Doctrine was reiterated by Secretary of State Root in 1906, in replying to a petition requesting the United States to take action to prevent the persecution of the Armenians by the Turkish Government: "By the unwritten law of more than a century, we are," he said, "debarred from sharing in the political aims, interests, or responsibilities of Europe, just as by the equally potential doctrine, now nearly a century old, the European powers are excluded from sharing or interfering in the political concerns of the sovereign states of the Western Hemisphere." Secretary Olney had previously held in his note to Lord Salesbury during the Venezuela boundary dispute in 1895-6, that: "American non-intervention in Europe implied European non-intervention in America."

3. Blockade and starve into submission any nation or group of nations that opposes this empire control program.

Ideology No. 1 did not arise until the 1890's and was the expression of the vision of Cecil Rhodes of a one-government warless world. It caught the fancy of many other dreamers and idealists who saw in it a solution of the periodical wars of the world, and failed to see in it the seed of gigantic wars of the future in the opposition of powerful races who would decline to recognize the fantastic doctrine of the racial superiority of the Anglo-Saxon and of his pre-ordained destiny to rule all the races of the earth. This doctrine was an integral part of Ideology No. 1 and was definitely expressed by one of its leading American proponents, the late William Allen White, newspaper publisher, in these words: "It is the destiny of the pure Aryan Anglo-Saxon race to dominate the world and kill off or else reduce to a servile status all other inferior races."

Only a very limited number of the British ruling class can make any pretentions of being "pure Aryan Anglo-Saxons," as the average Englishman is a mixture of all the races on earth, of all the oppressed peoples and fugitives who crossed the waters of the British Channel to the new free land beyond over a period of a thousand years; and of the British nobility itself a large proportion is Jewish. The Angles and the Saxons were Germans, and more of their descendants and relatives remained in Germany than migrated to England. The Merriam-Webster dictionary defines an Anglo-Saxon as a member of the mixed race which forms the English nation. Few people can trace all branches of their ancestry very far, and those that can trace it back to some worthy individual in any branch, are content to stop there and to accept that as the answer to their own pretentions; and when we note that Adolf Hitler was still a 23 year old common laborer on building construction at a time when the words of Mr. White received wide acclaim in Britain and America, we can reasonably ask who started all this hokum of the master race.

The American pilgrims and partners who entered the new secret ideology in 1897 knew that they were renouncing and abandoning the established isolationism of "America for the Americans" for a presumably bigger and better ideology, despite the fact that for another 45 years the pretension of Pan-Americanism was kept up, until the recent acquisition of absolute control over American foreign affairs made possible the deft substitution of global Ideology No. 1.

The Monroe Doctrine was promulgated in 1823 at a time when the newly formed British-French alliance of the international bankers was faced with a rising discontent in the vast Mohammedan world and when their fleets were needed to protect their holdings in the Near-east, the Middle-east and the Far-east. Its inception was greeted with derision by the British press, but no immediate overt move resulted, because an uprising in the

88

Greek Christian provinces of Turkey, nominal protector of Mohammedanism, had provided a suitable cause for intervention, and it was urgent to overcome the menace of the Mussulman first.

Due to her sympathy with the suppressed Greek Christians, Russia entered the war against Mohammedanism and on October 20, 1827, the allied British-French-Russian fleet destroyed the allied Mohammedan fleet at the Battle of Navarino. Having initiated Russia into the war with Turkey and Egypt, Britain and France withdrew from the conflict, and after Russia had defeated Turkey two years later, curtailed her victory to such an extent that Turkey emerged out of the conflict as a British ally.

This initiated the long-drawn friction with Russia which ended in the great Crimean War, in which Russia was totally defeated and disarmed in the Black Sea area in 1856, and the Russian influence in the power politics of Europe removed for one hundred years in the opinion of many prominent British statesmen and writers.

Thus the British interest had been actively engaged in other parts of the world for 33 years after the Monroe Doctrine had been initiated, but now they were able to turn their attention at last to America. A close business relationship had grown up between the cotton-growing aristocracy of the southern states and cotton manufacturing England, and the southern states were swarming with British agents. Soon a great conspiracy arose among southern politicians, which erupted with the secession of South Carolina from the Union on December 20, 1860, followed by six more states in about one month. The conspirators raised armies and seized forts, arsenals, mints, ships and other National property. Members of the Cabinet actively engaged in crippling the Union, injuring the public credit and working to bankrupt the nation, with the apparently passive assent of President Buchanan. (*)

It was in this situation that the Republican dark-horse candidate Abraham Lincoln, victor in a four-cornered slave and anti-slave race for the Presidency, came into office on March 4, 1861. There had been a lot of bloodshed before Lincoln was inaugurated, but it is part of the American Fable that the first shot of the Civil War was fired at Fort Sumter on April 12, 1861.

In December, 1861, a large British, French and Spanish expeditionary force was landed at Vera Cruz in defiance of the Monroe Doctrine. This, together with direct British aid to the Confederacy, and the fact that the Confederate army was far better trained and armed than the Federal forces at the outset of the war, brought the fortunes of the North to a very low ebb; and every indication at this stage was that Britain was preparing to enter the war.

_____

(*) Illustrated Univ. History, 1878—page 504.

In this extremity, President Lincoln appealed to Britain's perennial enemy Russia for aid. When the document with this urgent appeal was given to Alexander II, he weighed it unopened in his hand and stated: "Before we open this paper or know its contents, we grant any request it may contain. On the day on which your President was inaugurated, we, Alexander II of Russia, signed the protocol which liberated twenty-three million serfs. Abraham Lincoln, President of the United States, has freed four million slaves. Therefore, whatever he asks of Russia, Russia will grant, for Alexander II will not be a factor in the enslavement of any man." Unannounced, a Russian fleet under Admiral Lisiviski steamed into New York harbor on September 24, 1863, and anchored there; while the Russian Pacific fleet under Admiral Popov arrived at San Francisco on Oct. 12th. Of this Russian action, Gideon Wells said: "They arrived at the high tide of the Confederacy and the low tide of the North, causing England and France to hesitate long enough to turn the tide for the North."

As a matter of fact, Russian interest had made the entire matter a subject of the Concert of Europe, and Britain had already been obliged to withdraw from the Mexican venture and leave the same to Napoleon III by the dangerous reaction in Europe, and the rising tide of Liberalism and anti-Imperialism at home; while the imperialistic aspirations of Napoleon III were shortly after drastically snuffed out by Bismarck, to be followed by 43 years of relative peace in Europe.

The British interference had caused a furious resentment in the United States, immortalized by the words of the song: "In every battle kill our soldiers by the help they give the foe;" and when a demand for payment of direct and contingent damages due to this interference was rejected by Britain in 1869, war again was close. The controversy dragged out, however, and did not again break out until February 1872, when a Court of Arbitrations met and the British Arbitrator, Sir Alexander Cockburn, violently objected to the consideration of claims for indirect or contingent damages. After several months of futile argument, the United States gave up this part of its claims, and on September 6, 1872, was awarded very nominal damages of fifteen and one-half million dollars.

Napoleon III withdrew his troops from Mexico shortly after the end of the Civil War upon demand of the United States; and the Mexican Emperor placed on the throne created by him, Archduke Maximilian of Austria, was executed June 19, 1867.

An interesting sidelight on the relationship between certain members of the British and Southern aristocracies and elite of Civil War days, appears from the large part played by Joseph E. Wheeler, renowned Confederate and Spanish-American War cavalry general, in his activities in the subsequent subversion of the now firmly established and invincible ideology of the Monroe Doctrine and Pan-Americanism to Ideology No. 1; for Joe Wheeler was a principal organizer of the Pilgrim secret society of International Finance, as related by Sir Harry Brittain in his "Pilgrim Partners."

The argument was expressed by Chauncey M. Depew, founder vice-president of the Pilgrims, that incontrollable overproduction would inevitably lead America back to stagnation and poverty, a very potent and fearful prospect at a time when it was just barely creeping out of the horror of the giant depression of the 1890's, but for its entry in what is herein indicated for purpose of brevity as Ideology No. 1.

In denial, former Congressman Towne in his speech "Lest We Forget," condemning American participation in the grand plan of International Finance to immediately eliminate Germany and Russia from the markets of the Far East with the aid of Japan, said of the theory af remediless over-production which supplied the justification of this intrigue: "When men freeze at the mouth of a coal mine and starve in front of a bake shop, when the per capita consumption of wheat decreases as population multiplies, when millions of our citizens lack roof and raiment, to say that there is an overproduction of the necessaries of life is both an economic absurdity and an arraignment of our American civilization at the bar of humanity and justice . . ."

At about the same time the Rev. Henry Van Dyke stated in a sermon: ". . . if Americans do not thirst for garrison duty in the tropics they must be bought or compelled to serve . . . to wilfully increase our need of military force by an immense and unnecessary extension of our frontier of danger is to bind a heavy burden and lay it upon the unconscious backs of future generations of toiling men . . . If we go in among them we must fight when they blow the trumpet."

Further comment on the desperate expedient adopted by the exponents of the "Full Dinner Pail" to fulfill their campaign promise and to overcome the terrible depression of the 90's appears in an article written by the late Samuel Gompers, President of the American Federation of Labor, in which he stated:- "A 'foreign war as a cure for domestic discontent' has been the device of tyrants and false counselors from time immemorial, but it has always lead to a Waterloo, a Sedan, to certain decadence and often utter ruin."

The above statements are to be found among over thirty great speeches and articles against the great intrigue of 1897 in William J. Bryan's "Republic or Empire?" published in 1899; and the American statesmen and educators whose they are, proved to have been great and true prophets in the crucible of 45 years; but they are prophets without honor in their own country, for to revive their words is to expose facts that those in interest want forgotten.

There is no interval in American history so obscure as that between the secret agreement of 1897 and the tipping of the scales in favor of the British-French division of Africa by Theodore Roosevelt at the Conference of Algeciras in 1906. The second Hay-Pauncefote Treaty, one of the greatest political horse-trades of history, was concluded November 18, 1901, in order to obtain the British-French "permission" to build the Panama Canal; but writers and historians of this era are, in general, very vague as to the nature of the deal by which the noxious British restrictions, among other prohibiting the fortification and defense of the Canal Zone, were eliminated from the first treaty of Feb. 5, 1900; which the U. S. Senate had rejected.

John K. Turner in "Shall It Be Again?" published 1922, covers the fact that secret diplomacy was employed by our presidents in precisely the same manner as our allies and enemies employed it; and there is little question that the two presidents who have deplored secrecy and hypocrisy the loudest, Theodore Roosevelt and Woodrow Wilson, were among the most prolific users of secret diplomacy. (See footnote.)

In accordance with the British rule of Empire: "Establish naval bases around the world to control the sea and commerce lanes;" Britain maintains a mighty array of island approaches to the Americas, and while the United States is now permitted air bases on some of these islands; these air bases, constructed at immense cost, must all be returned to become the property of the "Crown" or "City" after the war is over. Despite her rebuff in America after the Civil War, Britain has tolerated, but never accepted, the ideology of Pan-Americanism and the Monroe Doctrine. She has insisted on her full rights as the dispenser of the "Freedom of the Seas," and therefore building of the Panama Canal required a "material quid pro quo" for the interests of the British-French Financial oligarchy, which in all probability involved our entry into Ideology No. 1, support of their contentions at Algeciras, participation in World War I, and many more things.

There has been fostered an illusion that some nations have certain

---

In "From Isolation to Leadership," published 1918, John Holladay Latane, Professor of American History in the Johns Hopkins University, states in regard to the Conference at Algeciras in 1906, (page 76): "The facts in regard to America's part in this conference have never been fully revealed. There is nothing in any published American document to indicate that the participation of our representatives was anything more than casual. Andre Tardieu, the well-known French publicist, who reported the conference and later published his impressions in book form, makes it evident that President Roosevelt was a positive factor in the proceedings. He states that at a critical stage of the conference the German Kaiser sent several cablegrams to President Roosevelt urging him to modify his instructions to Mr. White.

"There can be no doubt that our participation in the Moroccan conference was the most radical departure ever made from our traditional policy of isolation. *Roosevelt's influence was exerted for preserving the balance of power in Europe.* As we look back upon the events of that year we feel, in view of what has happened that he was fully justified in the course he pursued. *Had his motives for participating in the conference been known at the time, they would not have been upheld either by the Senate or by public opinion. There are many serious objections to secret diplomacy, but it cannot be done away with even under a republican form of government until the people are educated to a fuller understanding of international politics.*

established rights in their ideologal aims and position, while others are law breakers. To give body to this allusion, there is usually added positive reference to International Law. Prof. Edwin J. Clapp developed in his "Economic Aspects of The War," mentioned hereinbefore, that there is no such thing as International Law. International Law had consisted of the interpretation of the successive interlocking international agreements made by the nations of the world in meetings assembled under the provisions of the Concert of Europe. The Concert of Europe operated from about 1813 until it was laid to its final rest in the waters of Manila Bay on the morning of May 1, 1898, by International Finance, after it already had been reduced previously to a rather feeble shadow by the same forces. International Finance thereafter salvaged as many of the interpretations of the Concert of Europe as were useful, and added other desirable interpretations by "Order-in-Council," as needed, as largely developed by Prof. Clapp.

The eminent British engineer, scientist and inventor, Arthur Kitson, Chairman of the Committee of Science and Arts of Franklin Institute of Philadelphia for ten years, and author since 1894 of a number of profound works attacking the fallacy of the "Money Power" and of "Economic Depressions" and of that menacing over-production of food and merchandise side by side with the most dire want condemned by former Congressman Charles A. Towne forty-five years ago as an "economic absurdity," in an article in the New Britain Magazine of London, of June 20, 1934; cited a devastating assertion by David Lloyd George that "Britain is the slave of an international financial bloc;" quoted words written by Lord Bryce that: "Democracy has no more persistent or insidious foe than the money power . . .;" pointed out Mr. Winston Churchill as one of the supporters of International Finance; and stated: "Questions regarding the Bank of England, its conduct and its objects, are not allowed by the Speaker." (of the House of Commons).

Mr. Kitson stated further: "Democracy in this country has become a farce! The real governing power is not at Westminster nor at Downing Street, but rests partly in Threadneedle Street and partly in Wall Street, New York! There sits every day in the Bank of England premises, during banking hours, a representative of the Federal Reserve Board of New York for the purpose of advising and even instructing the Governor of the Bank regarding his policies. When the Governor and Deputy-Governor were invited to testify before the recent MacMillan Committee, the Governor introduced Mr. Sprague — his American adviser!"

This American ascendancy in the affairs of the British Empire has so far cost the American people a vast sum of money, but this money seems to be in the nature of a purchase of an interest in that Empire, for exuberant American post-war planners are openly making plans which seem to proclaim

93

them the successors of those controlling the British Empire; themselves the jugglers of world power which would make certain that the American people would not only be the principal participants in the major wars of the world, but would also take a part in all the minor wars of the British Empire and the world; that borrowing the words of the English Professor Cramb: "Scarcely a sun will set in the years to come, which will not look upon some American's face dead in battle—dead not for America—dead to satisfy the ambitions of power-crazed men."

Mr. Haxey in his "England's Money Lords M.P." covers at some length the Anglo-German Fellowship and its high Tory members, among whom is listed Sir Harry Brittain of the Pilgrims. Lord Mount Temple, son-in-law of the great Jewish financier Sir Ernest Cassel, was at one time a Chairman of this organization. Another member, Lord Redesdale, father-in-law of Sir Oswald Mosley, stated in 1936 that he was one of those who considered it high time that some arrangement should be made whereby Germany should have some of her Colonial territory restored to her. Many highly placed Germans were close to these high members of International Finance and Conservatism and this secret organization may well be prepared to function in any situation where the upstart amateur American planners in their delusions of grandeur forget their junior status in the organization of the *master planners of an eventual British dominated world;* for, as developed by Prof. Spykman on page 103 of "America's Strategy in World Politics," the game of the balance of power permits no enduring friendships. He concludes that British tactics have invariably made the friend of today the opponent of tomorrow. The possibility of the Anglo-German Fellowship taking over from the Pilgrims may not be too remote with only a slight shift in British home politics.

The post-war plans of other countries with large natural resources, particularly those of China and Russia as now indicated, are being shaped to follow the American plan of prosperity by keeping out the goods of other countries in order to encourage their own industry and wealth by the aid of a high tariff wall or some equivalent measure; then to use every possible means of outselling other lands in foreign markets. China, free after 100 years of British overlordship and encirclement, will be a mighty competitor with her intelligent and industrious population. Her bankers and businessmen rank among the most able in the world. Her tariff wall has always been among the highest, but heretofore a large part of the customs has been in British hands, and British agents have disbursed the funds collected by them under the provisions of that part of the "Laws of England" (Vol. 23, p. 307, par 641) quoted in the footnotes of Chapter V.

According to an article "How Fast Can Russia Rebuild?" by Edgar Snow in the Saturday Evening Post of Feb. 12, 1943, Russia has made some far-reaching post-war plans which apparently do not include any markets in Russia for American made goods; which do definitely propose to equal and surpass the United States in every line of production before 1960. They plan to sell these goods in the same markets for which the United States is fighting, and it would seem that the Commissar of the Russian Foreign Trade Monopoly may have a considerable edge over American private enterprise.

In attempting to meet this foreign competition the United States would be unable to take independent action as a member of Ideology No. 1. It would have to consult and await the views of its British and other associates, and abide by the decision of other peoples. So handicapped, the crash of the American standard of living to the common level, conjectured as a possibility by Professor Usher in "The Challenge of the Future," published in 1916, is moving into the range of nearby probability; and many of the startling postulates advanced by Professor Usher in his works of 1913, 1915 and 1916, have already moved into the realm of fact.

The American standard of living was well illustrated in a discourse entitled "What the Machine Has Done to Mankind" presented at the 1937 Annual Meeting of the Western Society of Engineers by James Shelby Thomas, in which he stated that with only 7% of the population of the world we produce half of the food crops of this planet, that half of the world's communication system belongs to us, that we use half of the world's coffee and tin and rubber, 3-4th's of its silk, 1-3 of the coal and 2-3 of all the crude oil in the world; and then goes on to defend the cause of the machine against those that blame on it some of the ills of the world.

The American people lead the world in science and invention, but their geopolitical sense has not kept in step with developments, so there is cause to fear that in that respect the United States is in the precarious predicament of the prehistoric dinosaur whose body grew too large for its head. Instead of ascribing the marvelous prosperity of the United States to its self-sufficiency and its isolation from the wars and the crushing burden of armaments and taxation that have kept the people of Europe in endless and hopeless poverty, a false theory has been created that this prosperity depends on eliminating other peoples from the markets of the world; a resurrection of the barbarous conceptions of biblical times in which conquering hosts put whole peoples to the sword.

It is said that only a few dozen men in the world know the nature of money; and therefore these few men are allowed to practice the manipulation of money and of that mysterious commodity known as credit as a mystic rite, despite the fact that their machinations cause recurrent giant depressions in which many of the life savings of the people are lost, and cause recurrent gigantic bloodshed in which the people must sacrifice their lives to protect the manipulators from the fury of those nations and peoples who have been

95

their victims; and despite the fact that eminent students of high business, financial and social position, such as Vincent C. Vickers and Arthur Kitson, have condemned this money system as a fraud; have condemned the men who manipulate it as super-criminals and traitors to their own lands and peoples, and have condemned the recurring economic depressions and wars as the deliberate products of the money power.

The deranged conception that a nation to retain its prosperity and to escape return to stagnation and poverty, must always continue to sell more than it buys, most certainly demands that some other nation or nations must always buy more than they sell. Once these other nations have exhausted their surplus gold and credits this process must end, and the account must be added up and balanced. To keep up American-British preponderance of sales the process was artifically extended and aggravated by the extension of immense credits by International Finance to those countries drained of gold, adding an immense interest burden to their already seriously strained economy, and thus paving the way to repudiation, anarchy and dictatorship as a release from an impossible dilemma.

The power of International Finance rests upon the doctrine of government advanced by Niccolo Machiavelli, which holds that any means, however unscrupulous, may be justifiably employed in order to maintain a strong central government; and this doctrine has always been used as a vindication and the mandate of imperialists and dictators, and it cannot gain a foothold unless the forces of freedom have become undermined and are no longer able to offer open opposition. (See footnote.)

The people could regain their power by voting into office men definitely on record in opposition to International Finance. The power of International Finance could then be curbed by prohibiting any interchange of international values or credits by any private agency, and the prohibition of any intercourse or dealings by any government representative with any private agency, such as the Bank of England, in any foreign country. Foreign trade could be conducted under the supervision of a Commission formed of representatives of all nations, operating a central bank dealing only in credits arising out of commodity sales and purchases; permitting no interchange of gold or paper credits except under its strict supervision. By this means no nation would be able to sell more values than they are able to buy. The United States

---

In a lengthy well-detailed article "Let's Quit Pretending" in the Saturday Evening Post of December 18, 1943, Demaree Bess described the extent of the deceptions and the contradictions by which "propagandists" and the Government have kept the American people in the dark as to their foreign position over a period of years. He described how far the American Government was actively engaged in war with unconditional commitments to foreign governments and foreign political factions months before Pearl Harbor. He dwelt also on the fears of many Americans that a "bad mess" may result in this country out of the expenditure of American lives and money to bring about a world such as is apparently in the making.

96

would not be affected very adversely as will be readily apparent from an examination of foreign trade statistics over the past 45 years, in short our foreign trade was never very important; and would actually profit by trade with a revived Europe. Nations with large populations and small natural resources and territory, being obliged to import heavily, would also be able to sell in proportion; thus overcoming a large part of the lack in self-sufficiency. Debtor nations to be permitted excess sales to liquidate their obligations, and their creditors to be penalized equivalent values in sales until the debts are liquidated. Other affairs between nations to be subject to a semi-formal organization such as the late Concert of Europe, electing its own temporary presiding officers and allowing no man, or nation, or group of nations a definite ascendancy; and subjecting each representative to qualification as to personal connection with any power or pressure group.

As matters stand now, with the end of the war considered by many as a near-by possibility, there is little talk of a "Peace Conference" or of some world organization, such as the League of Nations of the last war, to take over after the war. It appears that the end of the war is to find the defeated in the position of apprehended criminals coming up to the bar to hear their sentence from the lips of the dictators of the "United Nations;" with subsequent events in the hands of "Post-War Planners."

In the penetrating classic, "The American Commonwealth," published in 1888, James Bryce stated: "The day may come when in England the question of limiting the at present all but unlimited discretion of the executive in foreign affairs will have to be dealt with, and the example of the American Senate will then deserve and receive careful study." A little reflection will indicate that the contrary has occurred, that the United States has become a subject of the "Laws of England."

XIV

CONCLUSION

December 31, 1945 (2nd Edition)

The foregoing matter of the first edition was written about two years ago and the "One World" camarilla has since advanced very close to its planned objective as may be apparent from a copy of the "Articles of Agreement of the International Monetary Fund and International Bank for Reconstruction and Development," adopted at Bretton Woods, New Hampshire, July 22, 1944; which appeared in "International Conciliation, No. 413" dated September, 1945, a booklet issued by the Carnegie Endowment for International Peace with a preface by Dr. Nicholas Murray Butler.

The following sentences were selected from Article IX, Sections 1 to 9:

The fund shall possess full juridical personality.

Shall have immunity from judicial process.

Property and assets of the Fund, wherever located and by whomever held, shall be immune from search, requisition, confiscation, expropriation, or any other form of seizure by executive or LEGISLATIVE ACTION.

The archives shall be held inviolable.

. . . all property and assets shall be free from restrictions, regulations, controls, and moratoria of any nature.

The officers and personnel shall be immune from legal processes, immigration restrictions, alien registration requirements, and national service obligations; shall be immune from taxation and customs duties, immune from liability for taxes and duties.

No taxation of any kind shall be levied on any obligation or security, dividend or interest of the Fund.

This is obviously merely a precise rewording of the ambiguous provisions of the "Laws of England;" which, as variously developed hereinbefore, have placed the Bank of England over and above LEGISLATIVE ACTION heretofore, and made of it a sovereign world supergovernment; with the House of Commons prohibited even from discussing its activities, while the House itself was subject to the orders of "the executive" as to the legislation required by "The City."

Thus the denizens of The City, who have heretofore been obliged to exist in furtive secrecy in the dark recesses of the Bank of England, are now able to abandon their lair to move into the magnificent structure of "One World" omnipotence erected by their henchmen, to rule their world realm in recognized and sublime dignity.

The British economy is burdened with numerous vested privileges which entitle their "proprietors" to everlasting perquisites out of the public funds. This "systemé" is recognized and supported by the British Labor Party, whose leadership is patently fraudulent and is neither Liberal or Labor, as is apparent from its naive proposal to buy the now empty shell of the Bank of England from its owners with money to be procured from the people of the United States. That even the administration of the British public treasury admittedly comes into this category of private perquisite should be quite significant.

But these vested perquisites of the British ruling class blanket the earth, and are asserted with such nonchalant and brazen affrontery as to overawe dispute into dumbfounded inaction, and they include practically every basic commodity of world commerce and industry, be it international news, shipping and port rights, canal tolls, coaling monopolies, cartel control over rubber (to all appearance even to its manufacture in this country), colonial trade restrictions, or dictatorial disposition over vast segments of colonial empire.

The weapons of the "systemé" are bully and bluff, bribery and besmear, and the bewilderment of the public by being able through control or intimidation of public sources of information to accuse each of the successive challengers of "One World" of its own ideology of world rule and exploitation; and to convict them of its own lies and crimes.

The modern dictators were the deliberate creations of international finance to plunge the world into that chaos out of which alone it would be possible to fashion "One World." It was first necessary to make the people of all the world tractable and obedient to these plans in a successive process involving in their planned turn the people of the United States. The method by which this could be achieved was indicated 25 years ago by a leading financial organ in these words: "When through process of law, the common people have lost their homes, they will be more tractable and more easily governed through the influence of the strong arm of Government, applied by the general power of wealth under control of leading financiers."

The structure of world supergovernment revealed hereinbefore in documented step by step detail receives almost daily verification in the news of greedy Imperialistic contest for the loot made possible by American victory. The mask of sanctimonious hypocrisy usually assumed in these grabs has been largely dropped in the need for haste to beat Communism or Nationalism to the plunder in most of the lands of the world.

The Chicago Tribune of Dec. 1, 1945, on its front page carried the inside story of Senator Moore of Oklahoma, in which is made public the fact that the mystic British Government owns vast holdings in 80 of the largest American industrial corporations, among which are listed 434,000 shares of General Motors and 315,000 shares of Standard Oil of Indiana. At a moment when the market has reached at 14 year peak, the "smart" money of the foreign clique which engineered the market excess of 1929 and thereby broke the back of the American economy, again overhangs the market.

The American public was blindly led to the slaughter then like so many sheep being driven up the ramp at the abattoir, with endless years of ruin and fear to follow for the millions. Its government is now likewise being deliberately led into economic disaster, for history records that every excess is followed by reaction in direct proportion to its extremity.

Lord Keynes is termed the world's most influential living economist and the key man of Britain's treasury, in an article by Noel F. Busch in the Sept. 17, 1945, issue of Life. Mr. Busch records that, as economic adviser to the Chancellor of the Exchequer, he had come to Washington to obtain a satisfactory substitute for Lend-Lease. Lord Keynes, who is a neighbor in Cambridge of Lord Rothschild, and who is a director of the Bank of England, and who was the chief financial adviser of David Lloyd George in drafting the financial clauses of the Versailles Treaty, is credited with being indirectly responsible for the New Deal policy of endless spending, and is revealed as the originator of the Bretton Woods plan.

The financial clauses of the Versailles Treaty are perhaps the most fantastically unreal parts of this most perfidious instrument ever devised, and from a practical standpoint comprise merely so much gibberish. It is then significant to note that the leading protagonist of these clauses is described 25 years later as being consistently inconsistent in his economic concepts, with a remarkable facility to contradict himself whenever this seems appropriate. It is further developed that Keynes, who is a director also of a number of leading financial corporations of "The City," should not alone be blamed for the 1929 American market crash, which it is indicated he naturally foresaw a long time in advance, and out of which he personally profited immensely.

On Dec. 9, 1945, Representative White of Idaho, cited voluminous statistics showing Great Britain has nearly 50 billion dollars worth of assets, among them 2½ billion dollars invested in American industry. There is no indication of any comparable American holdings of British industry, nevertheless the British Government demanded and was awarded several billions of dollars on a plea of poverty, backed up with a threat of economic reprisal. The British Government had already been given about 30 billion dollars, much of it for non-war purposes and for reasons that were obviously incorrect

100

and spurious, to the stage where the American economy is apparently out of control and rapidly moving to destruction.

Repr. White developed that while this lend-lease was under way to an alleged bankrupt British Government, that British Government was able, by a financial mumbo-jumbo which does not permit the right hand to know what the left hand is doing, to purchase 600 million dollars of American gold; and that, in addition, it was lend-leased 300 million ounces of silver. Neither International Finance or any other system of finance disposes over any mystical or magical formula, unless the periodical watering and unwatering of money values can be rated as such; and all these mysterious financial convolutions in the end boil down to the simplest of simple arithmetic; to the continued plunder of the American economic system with the planned purpose of its destruction.

Two interesting accounts appeared on the front page of the Chicago Tribune of Dec. 6, 1945. In one, Maj. Gen. Patrick J. Hurley, former special ambassador to China, charges career men in the state department with sabotaging American foreign policy by fighting for the imperialistic designs of Great Britain, Holland and France; nations, as developed hereinbefore, whose financial systems are dominated by The City. The other account is of the first dinner meeting of the Pilgrim Society since the outbreak of the war, in which it is identified as a "hands across the sea organization." It recounts that both Labor Prime Minister Atlee and the lord high chancellor of the Laborite government, Lord Jowitt, were among the speakers; and that Lord Jowitt had stated he had greeted the Japanese attack on Pearl Harbor, in which 3,000 Americans died, with "thank God for that." Prime Minister Atlee lauded the United States "for having conquered all and given great satisfaction to everybody here."

It is likely that this dinner meeting was held at the ultra exclusive club of the Conservatives, the renowned Carlton Club, traditional meeting place of the Pilgrims. According to accounts, this club purveys the very finest in service of any club in all the world. It seems strange to find alleged Laborites and Liberals as honored guests at this rededication function of their alleged oponents.

The same newspaper in the same issue of Dec. 6, 1945, entitles its leading editorial, "Senators Who Lied;" and then develops that Senators Connally and Vandenberg welshed three months later on the pledges they and their fellow delegate, John Foster Dulles, associate of the American Pilgrim president, Dr. Nicholas Butler, on the board of the Carnegie Endowment for International Peace, had made to the American people at San Francisco.

On Dec. 10, 1945, Gen. Hurley charged that the United Kingdom Commercial Corporation, a profit making corporation owned by the British government, was selling American lend-lease supplies in 18 countries and keeping the money. This charge was termed "utterly fantastic" by Dean Acheson, Undersecretary of State, who stated further that Gen. Hurley never had understood the lend-lease system in the middle east. Mr. Hurley testified in a hearing of the Senate Foreign Relations Committee on this date in part, as follows: "The British corporation was selling American automobile tires. I required the corporation to put the money in the bank to pay for them. And I am told the money was given back to the corporation later by Mr. Acheson."

Gen. Hurley is an eminent attorney, soldier and statesman, who was awarded the distinguished service medal as a general officer in World War I, and who served as Secretary of War in the last Republican administration. His charge, in effect, of treachery and treason, was insolently and contemptuously dismissed as mere exaggeration and lack of ordinary intelligence.

Franklin D. Roosevelt asserted that economists have revised their fundamental conceptions every few years to conform with the trend of economic tides. But our leading legal lights have moved with the celerity of weather vanes in revising their conceptions and interpretations and application of basic Constitutional law in order to remain compatible with their status on the public payroll. It would seem that the weasel worded interpretations of leading jurists threaten to undermine and bring discredit, not only to its practitioners, but to the entire American legal structure.

The Constitution of the United States is written in plain words, and these words were intended to apply in their broadest meaning. It is not written in legal terminology, and does not require and should not tolerate the layer upon layer of pseudo legal inhibitions with which it has been encrusted, with each successive layer drawing increasing sustenance from preceding layers; to the end, that the Internationalist clique is now able to nullify any part of it at will.

Opposed by only 7 votes, the United States Senate, whose members are incidentally largely lawyers, voted to surrender part of the functions of the Senate and to set aside part of the Constitution of the United States, that Constitution which alone is authority for the existence of a Senate, and to delegate these functions to a foreign organization of world government; which by the provisions cited previously herein proposes thereafter to be no longer subject to any legislative action.

Members of the Congress have been subject to an intensive process of intimidation. Leading Nationalists were nearly all Republicans and many of them were already eliminated in 1932 to 1936. The lot of the transgressor against the plans of the "One Worlders" has been a hard and unhappy one since then. More of the most outstanding Nationalists were eliminated by

102

lavish use of the taxpayers money for vicious smear campaigns. The American people have been literally drugged by propaganda. Big lies have become exposed, but have been simply wiped out by bigger lies. Of these bigger lies, such as his "Give us the tools" and other monstrous exaggerations, Winston Churchill has nonchalantly observed that he lied because it was necessary.

The International clique would obviously attempt to frustrate counter attack on their astonishing and complicated pseudo legal structure of encroachment, by guiding this attack into the groove of procrastination, indirection, capriciousness and pure duplicity which has become a mark of American legal procedure in matters of this kind, and which made even the conviction of city gang leaders operating with the connivance of their own legal talent nearly impossible. This would mean that the finely limned maze of legal duplicity designed by them would have to be laboriously retraced and unsnarled, with scant chance of success.

American jurisprudence has become a ponderous and pompous tool of frustration of justice, in which legal technicalities permit the introduction of vast masses of matter unrelated to the direct issue and so permit the issue to be submerged. As officers of the court, the legal fraternity is accustomed to glibly interject its own versions to obscure the real issue and long practical observation indicates that no matter how obviously unreal they are, they seldom meet with rebuke from the court. It deliberately insults and belittles the public in the role of witness and puts on a show of extravagant professional superiority, not assumed by the members of any learned profession, in what can be termed pure judicial arrogance. The abominations of mass trials, which the legal profession has tolerated with but slight protest, can well be laid on its doorstep.

To cut this Gordian knot of organized and disorganized frustration, and to reduce this complex situation to its least common denominator, it would seem that the Constitution of the United States speaks for itself directly and needs no interpretations or interpreters; that the morning after the people have awakened to their peril and have elected a Congress of American Nationalists, these things and secret world orders will have ceased. The fantastic structure of world wide plunder and exploitation of humanity, masquerading as world law and order, is becoming more exposed day by day as its organizers climb further out on a limb, and it would then only await orderly disposition.

The principal purpose of the League of Nations was to validate Internationalist plunder with a spurious seal of world law and to gain time for its proponents to prepare for the inevitable World War II. The United Nations Organization is a product of the same group, in fact of many of the same men, and its purpose is precisely the same and to prepare for the inevitable World War III. The presumption with which the henchmen of this racket

103

are forcing their agents into control of still not fully subdued sovereign nations of Europe, Asia and South America, provides only a superficial preview of the endless bloody pacification that lies ahead, in which the money of the American taxpayer and the blood of American boys is to carry a large part of the cost.

The same group has succeeded in erasing even the memory of the Concert of Europe from the public mind, despite the fact that it functioned up to 1898 and that its agreements were still used as the basis for the Conference at Algeciras in 1906. In its approximately 85 year life it had erected an imposing structure of International Law. When the International clique sabotaged and destroyed this legitimate and effective structure of world law and order, they destroyed its International Law. The Internationalist pretention that laws substituted by them largely through the device of the "Order-in-Council" constitutes International Law rests on pure deceit.

The former precisely worded agreements between the nations made under the auspices of the Concert of Europe, blanketed the world. This machinery of arbitration was first undermined by secret bribery, then gradually disintegrated and demolished by "The City" through conspicuous and flagrant purchase of votes and general intimidation of the minor nations. "The City" administered the coupe de grace to the Concert of Europe with the formation of the overwhelming British-French-Dutch-Japanese-American imperialistic combine of 1897, which awarded the Philippine Islands and permission to build the Panama Canal to America as her quid pro quo.

Thus did International Finance degrade the world back to the law of the jungle. Then, to cover up, it immediately organized the abortive and make-believe Hague World Court in 1899 as a stopgap to confound humanity until its forces could be aligned for the now imminent and inevitable World War I. The decisive moment for this conflict came when the control of Italy had been bought for its agents, and Italy could be removed from its Triple Alliance with Germany and Austria-Hungary. The hallucination that Britain and its allies were then the innocent victims of an unprovoked and unanticipated attack is a triumph of the propaganda machine of "The City," and its almost absolute control over world news and sources of public information.

The utterly spurious nature of the Hague Court is readily evident from the few piddling and immaterial issues that were allowed to enter its hallowed portals for disposition in the period from 1899 to 1914, while none of the victims of the rampant British Imperialistic expansion of this period, and not one of the earth-shaking conflicts just prior to World War I, could gain a hearing.

The United States has been tricked into a position of boundless peril and foreign nations will continue to take advantage of its fallacious position by shameless and insolent demands for huge subsidies in the guise of loans; actually little more than blackmail of American power politicians, certain to lose their voice in world politics like did Mr. Wilson after World War I, unless they continue to give.

Great nations and great civilizations have been spent into cataclysm and chaos in the past, and we can read with foreboding the words of James J. Hill, railway empire builder, delivered in an address at Chicago on October 7, 1908, in which he said in part: "I need not remind you that our public credit, though vast, is not inexhaustible. Many of us have seen the day when it was strained to the breaking point. None of us knows when we may again need to rely upon it and when its strength or weakness will determine whether the nation is to live or to die. Of all our resources, perhaps, this one should be guarded with most jealous care; first because we can never know in advance where exhaustion begins. The earth and its products tell us plainly about what we may expect of them in the future; but credit is apparently unlimited at one moment and in collapse at the next. The only safe rule is to place no burdens upon it that may be avoided; to save it for days of dire need . . . .

"Search history and see what has been the fate of every nation that abused its credit. It is the same, only more awful in its magnitude and its consequences, as that of the spendthrift individual. And it will profit us nothing to conserve what we have remaining of the great national resources that were the dower of this continent unless we preserve the national credit as more precious than them all. WHEN IT SHALL BE EXHAUSTED THE HEART OF THE NATION WILL CEASE TO BEAT."

(The End)

INDEX

9 781585 092628